TWIST OF GOLD

Michael Morpurgo

TWIST OF GOLD

adapted by Simon Reade

OBERON BOOKS
LONDON

WWW.OBERONBOOKS.COM

First published in 2012 by Oberon Books Ltd
521 Caledonian Road, London N7 9RH
Tel: +44 (0) 20 7607 3637 / Fax: +44 (0) 20 7607 3629
e-mail: info@oberonbooks.com
www.oberonbooks.com

A catalogue record for this book is available from the British Library.

ISBN: 978-1-84943-206-1

Cover image by Pictureguy

Printed and bound by CPI Group (UK) Ltd, Croydon, CR0 4YY.

For Miles, Becky, Izzy & Ben

THE STORY

Ireland. 1847.

Driven out by starvation, plague and the occupying English, Sean (14) and his sister Annie (11) leave their Mother on her deathbed and adventure across the Atlantic to America in pursuit of their father. They take with them their torc, a twist of beaten gold, the golden necklace that has been the lucky talisman in their family for generations. Braving shipwreck, Boston winter, a mean-eyed bounty hunter on the wagon trail and the desolate prairies of the Wild West, they play the fiddle and dance a jig across the New World to the fertile pastures of Grass Valley, California. They are helped and supported on their eventful journey by characterful benefactors – and hindered by rogues whose greed is sparked by a glimpse of their twist of gold. It is Annie and Sean's resourcefulness, tenacity and courage in the face of adversity that keeps their spirits up and their hopes alive and sustains them on their journey into adulthood.

THE CHARACTERS

Ireland

ANNIE – nearly 11, gregarious, forthright, on the offensive when slighted. If called Sean's 'little sister' retorts 'I'm not little!' Blunt, curious, always asking questions; speaks her mind without always thinking through the consequences. Courageous. Irrepressible effervescence, which inspires all around her. Sister of:

SEAN – 14, positive, protective, proud of his sister. A good judge of character, responsible, loyal.

MOTHER – stoic, proud, pragmatic. Driven by love and hope and faith.

WILL – a Sergeant of the English Dragoons, a soldier of thirty years, but in Ireland 'I have seen and done things that turn my stomach with shame'. A jocular, belly-laughing giant of a man.

The Pelican

CAPTAIN MURRAY – English, embittered. Rules his America-bound emigrants' ship *The Pelican* like a tyrant. A man with a twisted soul, corrupted by the money to be made from the ever-hopeful Irish migrating to America. Cruel, greedy, but can turn on the charm.

MR BLUNDELL – *The Pelican*'s First Officer. Resembles a gargoyle more than a man, but not as fierce as he at first appears; tender-hearted beneath a rough exterior.

DONNELLY – a gangly, incorrigible, fiddle-playing young man from Sligo. Gentle, a joker. Full of confidence and good spirit, immodest yet selfless; seeking his fortune in America.

New England

MARTY – baccy-chewin' villager from the coast. Wry humour.

BOSTON CHANCER – a smile too broad to be believed.

MISS HENRY – imperious, domineering, formidable. Hard-hearted; short-haired. Beneath her bluster lies a heart of gold. Twin sister of:

MISS MARTHA – altogether more shy, soft-hearted and more obviously compassionate. Overwhelmed by her twin sister, Miss Henry. By contrast long-haired.

LIL' LUKE – a big, generous, optimistic black man, freed from the slavery in Virginia he ran away from years ago. General factotum to the spinster twins.

The Mid-West

BOUNTY HUNTER – trading in black men captured in the free north of America to take to the southern states. A cheat at cards, a mean-eyed man who smiles with his mouth only. He feeds off the unwary and the innocent.

COLONEL – the black sheep brother of Miss Henry and Miss Martha, who, thirty years ago, squandered a fortune, broke their father's heart, and was never forgiven by his sisters. Tall, elegant, leans on a silver-topped cane. Now tee-total. Owns a paddle-steamer which charts the Missouri river with a casino on board. A commanding presence, a natural born leader.

The Wild West

MATT COLBY – an honest Farmer, heading West on the wagon trail.

FRENCH CHARLIE – surly, whiskey-drinking, seasoned guide on the wagon-trail. Not to be trusted.

Sierra Nevada

SEAMUS FINN – Kerry-born, old man of the Mountain in the Sierra Nevada. Pursuing his dream of striking gold regardless of ridicule. Dotty but wise.

RED INDIAN CHIEF – fierce-looking but genteel; wily and wise.

THE CAST

This play can be performed by an ensemble of as few as six with doubling and cross-casting. Or it can be played by a company of up to thirty.

Sailors, Emigrants, Villagers, Crowds, Bystanders, Farmers, Grizzly Bears and other parts to be played by the ensemble.

SEAN and ANNIE might be cast from younger actors to differentiate them as children in an adult's world.

MUSIC

It would be neat to discover that the actor playing Sean and the actor playing Donnelly are both accomplished fiddle-players. Original music is welcome, but traditional airs, ballads and jigs can also be interwoven.

DESIGN

The scenes can be played with the minimal of design fuss. Bold lighting, a fabulous soundscape, and we're in a dwelling because we're told we are and there's the crackle of fire. Or we're on a ship because we've gone up a gang-plank; or climbed a ladder for a crow's-nest, and so on. Maybe everything is created organically from the same object, like a Wild West pioneer wagon?
Above all everyone should have as much fun in creating the play as the authors did in writing the novel and now the play. It's all in the storytelling.

Simon Reade, 2012

Twist of Gold was commissioned by Polka Theatre, where it was first performed on February 16th 2012.

Cast

Jo Castleton	Mother/Miss Martha/French Charlie
Trevor Allan Davies	Mr Blundell/Boston Chancer/ Bounty Hunter/Seamus Finn
Charlie Hamblett	Sean
Ian Harris	Will/Donnelly/Marty/Miss Henry/ Colonel/Red Indian Chief
Clive Llewellyn	Father/Captain Murray/Lil' Luke/ Matt Colby
Clare McMahon	Annie

Other parts played by members of the company.

Creative Team

Philip Wilson	*Director*
Max Jones	*Designer*
Philip Gladwell	*Lighting Designer*
Olly Fox	*Composer*
Max Perryment	*Sound Designer*
Richard Ryder	*Accent & Dialect Coach*

Crew

Dan Rainsford	*Production Manager*
Christopher Randall	*Technical Manager*
Nick Graham	*Stage Manager*
Emma McKie	*Deputy Stage Manager*
Lara Mattison	*Assistant Stage Manager*
Annie James	*Wardrobe Supervisor*
Lenny Hill	*Wardrobe Assistant*
Paula Hopkins	*Prop Maker*
Michalis Kokkoliadis	*Set Builder*
Mark Bramfitt	*Assistant Set Builder*
Lucy Ackland	*Scenic Artist*
Fani Louisa Parali	*Scenic Artist*

With thanks to: Michael Morpurgo, Miles Ketley, Gill McNeill, Philip Wilson and Jonathan Lloyd. And to Rose, Amy, Hazel, Otto and Alison.

PART I

Ireland. Autumn 1847.

SEAN (14, pale, thin, barefoot, in rags) and his sister ANNIE (nearly 11, barefoot, also in rags) support their frail MOTHER as they lay fresh, wild flowers on three small mounds of freshly dug, naked earth: the graves of their three dead siblings.

MOTHER: Danny, Mary, little Joe. A few more bites to eat and you'd not now be lying there in the ground. Oh my poor children.

MOTHER collapses, overwhelmed by grief, by hunger. SEAN comforts her.

*   *   *

The lights cross-fade to:

A brook. Drizzly autumn evening. Flies buzz irritably. SEAN fishes, hopelessly, with a line and baited hook. ANNIE is on lookout. She hears a horse cantering towards them on the opposite bank. An English DRAGOON – resplendent in scarlet cloak, golden plumed helmet and sword – dismounts.

DRAGOON: Whose waters are you poaching, children?

ANNIE and SEAN don't budge from their fishing.

SEAN: This is an Irish stream and Englishmen aren't welcome!

The DRAGOON looks at how SEAN is holding his line.

DRAGOON: You'll not catch any fish like that, and you look like you could do with a bite to eat.

He puts some biscuits into his handkerchief, ties it into a knot, and throws the modest bundle across the brook to the children. ANNIE is about to say 'thank you' – but thinks better of it.

WILL: My name is Will.

The Children say nothing. SEAN glares at WILL.

What's your name, boy? What do they call you at home?

Pause.

The biscuits. Maybe you've someone at home who'd be in need of them? Hm?

Pause.

I'm beginning to feel a bit stupid talking to myself.

ANNIE: Our Mother won't eat your English biscuits. She'd rather die.

SEAN: Hush, Annie.

WILL: I like a child who speaks their mind. Perhaps if she won't eat my biscuits then she'll eat this:

And he reaches inside his tunic to fetch out a small fish which he holds up by its tail.

Irish trout. Well, young lady, what do you think of that?

ANNIE: I'm not a young lady, I'm Annie O'Brien and my Mother says you've no business here, any of you. She says you're robbers and thieves.

A pause.

WILL: Is your mother sick?

SEAN: Everyone's sick.

ANNIE: She has the hunger.

Beat.

Brother Danny's dead and sister Mary's dead and little Joe died three weeks back.

WILL: And your father?

SEAN: Father's away, in 'Merica.

WILL: *(Gently.)* Tell your Mother I'm sorry about your brothers and sisters. I'd like to do what I can for you. For the three of you.

SEAN: How can we trust you?

WILL: How can *I* trust *you*? I don't even know your name, boy.

SEAN: Sean. I'm called Sean. Sean O'Brien.

WILL: Well, Sean, if you tell anyone about our meeting they'll lock me up and I'll never be able to see you again. So that's how you can trust me.

SEAN: Oh.

ANNIE: I'll trust you if you promise never to tumble our home and put us out.

WILL: Why would I do that?

ANNIE: You're an English soldier. We have no money for rent.

WILL: I won't tumble your home, Annie O'Brien. And as much as I can I'll see to it that no one else does either. Now, do you know how to cook a fish?

ANNIE: Slowly, so you don't burn away all the goodness.

WILL: That's right. *(He replaces his helmet.)*

ANNIE: Mister Soldier, is it not awful heavy having to wear such a hat as that?

WILL: It's what's inside your head that weighs heavy. Not what you wear on it. Do you understand me?

ANNIE: *(Boldly.)* No.

SEAN: Why are you helping us, Mister?

WILL: Sean, I'm a soldier. I have been a soldier for over thirty years. I've fought the world over for my Queen and for my country – that's my trade, and I do it well. But in Ireland I have seen and done things that turn my stomach with shame. Do you understand?

SEAN: I think so.

ANNIE: Well I don't.

WILL smiles.

WILL: To survive you must learn to live from the land.

ANNIE: That's what Mother says. But there's nothing left on the land to live from. Not now all you soldiers have taken it.

WILL: You may be right, Annie. But there's people dying in this country because they don't know where to look for their food, don't know how to catch it. You've all dug potatoes for so long, you've forgotten.

SEAN: That's not true! I know how to fish.

WILL: And how many fish have you caught, Sean?

> *Pause.*

Three? Four?

> *No response.*

Two?

SEAN: Not one.

WILL: And eels?

SEAN: Eels?

WILL: Eels are there in plenty if you can only catch them.

SEAN: How do you catch them?

WILL: When it's a still, dark night with no moonshine, and you can feel the light drizzle on the back of your neck as you stare into a black pool.

ANNIE: How does that catch an eel?

WILL: Keep your voice low, Annie. And when you laugh, laugh softly, else those eels will laugh too as they shoot off down river. An eel can hear you, you know.

ANNIE: No, I didn't know. Will: in your country, in England, do the people have enough food to eat?

WILL: The poor are always hungry, no matter where they live. But there are more poor living here and there is less food to go round, and more people stopping you from finding it.

ANNIE: People?

WILL: Soldiers.

ANNIE: English soldiers. Like you.

WILL: Yes, but not like me, Annie.

ANNIE: No, not like you.

SEAN: Before the potatoes died, we had food. Plenty of it. Sure, we went a bit short every year, just before the new potatoes were lifted – summer time – but then there were always the hens and the spring berries to keep us going.

WILL: Yes.

SEAN: Will we die do you think? Will everyone in Ireland die?

Pause.

ANNIE: *(To WILL.)* What's the matter?

WILL: Annie, Sean: I have to see your Mother.

SEAN: No.

WILL: Take me to your home.

ANNIE: It's a trick, Sean. Mother said it would be.

WILL: It's no trick, Annie.

ANNIE: She won't speak to you. She hates you.

WILL: Then I'll not come.

SEAN: We'll take your biscuits, mister, but not your fish. And we'll be thanking you.

WILL: Well. Goodbye.

* * *

SEAN and ANNIE make the journey home, accompanied by music. They enter their home: a spartan dwelling, no furniture, no bed; just fresh bracken on the hard earth floor. MOTHER, beneath her blanket, speaks without stirring.

MOTHER: *(Attempting to smile.)* Well, Sean dear: is it a salmon that you're bringing us this time?

SEAN: No salmon, Mother, but what would you say to a biscuit? A great, thick, oatmeal biscuit.

SEAN unwraps the tied handkerchief to reveal the biscuits – to his MOTHER's astonishment. She struggles to raise herself onto her elbows.

MOTHER: Three!

ANNIE: There'll be one for each of us, Mother. Can I eat it today? Can I eat all mine now?

MOTHER: Every bit, Annie dear. But eat slowly, for 'tis manna from heaven.

SEAN: Not heaven, Ma.

MOTHER: You didn't steal it, Sean?

SEAN: No!

ANNIE: *(Blurting it out.)* 'Tis a present from the English Army himself!

MOTHER: Sean?

SEAN: A Sergeant of the Dragoons. He brought his horse to the brook to water. He gave us the biscuits.

MOTHER: It's a trap! They followed you home. Annie: look out and see if there's anyone there.

SEAN: There's no one there, Mother. No one followed us. 'Tis food, Mother. If we don't eat, then there'll be none of us left when Father comes home to fetch us.

MOTHER: Have you not yet learned never to trust an English uniform? Do they not tumble homes, burn villages? While there are still fish in the rivers, rabbits in the field, we'll not be taking their biscuits –

SEAN: But Mother…

MOTHER: You're a good boy, Sean. Your father will be proud of you. And when he comes home to fetch us I will tell him how you've kept us in food when there's been no food. But I will not touch another of your English biscuits. I should die rather.

ANNIE: Don't say that. Rest now.

She tucks the blanket under her MOTHER's chin.

MOTHER: Oh, Annie: there's an anger and bitterness inside me that will hang over this land for hundreds of years after we're all gone.

MOTHER sleeps after her exertion. ANNIE stokes the peat fire, which roars.

ANNIE: Like Father said: 'The higher the chimney, the better it draws.'

SEAN: Truly, a wonderful creation.

ANNIE: *(Whispering to SEAN.)* Sean: why does Father not come back to us? It's more than a year now.

SEAN: *(Whispering.)* 'Tis a long way to America, Annie – and a long way back. And it's a very big place when you get there. He'll be finding us a farm, and a place to live, '*a paradise on earth…*'

FATHER 'delivers' the letter:

FATHER: '*…a paradise on earth, where the sun shines through the winter and there's food enough for everyone and plenty … I will be going as far West as the sun leads me. I will be following the sun all the way till it sets in a place they call Grass Valley, California. And when I have found Grass Valley I shall build us a house with the tallest chimney in all America, and then I will be coming back for you and we shall all be together again…*'

SEAN: Now that would take time, wouldn't it?

ANNIE: *(Whispering.)* Sure it would. But if he doesn't come soon, it will be too late.

SEAN: He'll come.

WILL bursts in.

Will!

ANNIE: English soldier! You followed us! You promised you wouldn't. Don't tumble our home, Mister.

WILL: I'm not going to harm you. I'm your friend. I had to follow you to find your home. I have to tell you and your Mother grave news.

MOTHER: *(Stirring.)* What can be more grave than the grave you'll bury us in, English soldier?

WILL: I've come to warn you.

MOTHER: Warn us of what?

WILL: There's a plague, a fever, sweeping the countryside. It's coming closer all the time.

MOTHER: *(Quietly.)* I know.

SEAN: You know?

MOTHER: There's always fever in Ireland. There always has been. It follows the hunger. It always has done.

WILL: *(Gently.)* Ma'am, this is a fever like no other. It wipes out whole villages.

MOTHER: No. It's the English who wipe out whole villages. And then burn them to the ground.

WILL: I regret that this is true, Ma'am. But now the Soldiers are torching the villages, on the orders of the authorities, to try to burn out the fever.

MOTHER: How can we trust you?

WILL: Your children asked me the same thing. I'm risking a court martial by being here.

MOTHER: Hunger is a terrible thing. Plague: terrible. We Irish have always known that. Do they not know that, your English 'authorities'? We ask for food, we beg for food and they send us work at tuppence a day, scarce enough to feed one child. And even if we could pay for food, there's no food to buy, so the people rise up and fight for it and they send more soldiers to put them down. And still the landlord we never see wants his rent paid. Rent for what? And if you don't pay the rent, the roof comes tumbling down over your head and you're left to die in a ditch.

Pause.

WILL: Ma'am, I can do nothing to put right all the great wrongs that have been done in this poor country. All I can do is to help you and your children. And there's only one thing to be done. You must leave, and leave now.

MOTHER: Leave and go where, sir?

WILL: Anywhere, but away from the Plague.

Pause.

MOTHER: Annie. Sit me up so that I can see this man better.

She does so.

Now, leave us children, I'll be wanting a few words with your soldier friend here. And don't be listening outside. There you go now.

ANNIE opens her mouth to ask a question –

No questions, Annie. Just do as I say.

They leave.

MOTHER: *(To WILL.)* You're right. They should leave.

WILL: 'They'?

MOTHER: I am dying, Soldier.

WILL: You are brave to admit it.

MOTHER: Death and the dying of it hold no fear for me. I know that my children Danny, Mary and Little Joe will be waiting for me on the other side. It is the parting from the living that troubles me.

WILL: Sean and Annie.

MOTHER: Sean and Annie. They should leave for America.

19

WILL: America?

MOTHER: It's where their father went, when the other children began to starve. He said that way there would be less mouths to feed…

FATHER 'delivers' his letter:

FATHER: '*…that way there will be less mouths to feed. But I will also be seeking our fortune, the O'Brien family fortune, seeking it out, surely, in bounteous America, the plentiful land of opportunity…*'

MOTHER: I should never have let him go.

WILL: Why not?

MOTHER: Because he left over a year ago. And he has yet to return.

Pause while this sinks in.

Mister Soldier, sir, will you be taking the children to the docks at Cork. The ships set sail from there to America, do they not?

WILL: They do. But for America? It's a fierce journey – especially for young children alone. And besides, the passage doesn't come cheap. These ships' captains want hard cash.

MOTHER: But we have none, sir.

WILL: And they'll not give you passage without it.

MOTHER: *(Defeated.)* No, sir.

WILL: I have money enough, Ma'am. Enough for the three of you. A soldier's pay is poor enough, but it is regular and I always keep some by me. You can get a passage for as little as…six pounds.

MOTHER: 'Tis too much. Why would you want to spend your money on us?

WILL: Your children make me smile and God knows I've done little enough of that since I've been over here.

MOTHER: I see now there may be some good in you.

WILL: Thank you Ma'am.

MOTHER: Even though you are an Englishman.

*   *   *

Outside, SEAN and ANNIE are by the graves of their brothers and sister.

ANNIE: Sean: if I ask you one question, will you promise me to answer true?

SEAN: I know what you're going to ask, Annie –

ANNIE: I'm old enough, I'm nearly eleven, and that's only three years younger than you. And she is my mother. I've a right to know.

SEAN: *(Softly.)* She is dying, Annie. And that's the truth of it. You know it without me telling you. We saw it with the others, the way their colour goes and the way they don't seem to want food even if it's there. They were just the same and they died.

ANNIE: Yes, I knew it, Sean. So we'll not be going anywhere, will we?

SEAN: She's too weak to move.

WILL has come outside.

WILL: Your Mother wishes to speak with you, children.

*   *   *

They enter their home.

MOTHER: Come closer, children. Tell them, Will. Tell them what you told me.

WILL: There's no hope for any of you in Ireland.

SEAN: Don't presume the future of our nation, mister!

WILL: If the hunger doesn't kill you, then the Plague will. I've seen it all over this country.

MOTHER: So that is why you must go.

SEAN: Go where?

MOTHER: To America. To Boston, where your father sailed to. And from where he went West.

ANNIE: But we must wait here for Father.

MOTHER: There's no time to wait, Annie.

ANNIE: Then you will come with us.

MOTHER: I shall be staying here, Annie. With Danny and Mary and little Joe.

WILL: We should go.

ANNIE: Why do you need to look after them and not us? Haven't enough of us passed away? Why won't you come with us?

MOTHER: You're always asking questions, Annie. Will you never just listen? Here. I want you to have this.

She takes a golden torc – a golden necklace – from her bosom.

The O'Briens were once a great clan, rich in land. We fought alongside kings. All we have now is you, Sean; and you, Annie – and this ancient torc of beaten gold, worn by the O'Brien chieftains one thousand years ago. Here. Wherever the O'Briens go, this torc must go with them. So long as we keep it, we will never forget who we are. You will wear it, Annie, and keep it hidden all the way to America. Put it round her neck, Sean. It will protect you both from the dangers you will be facing. It is the O'Brien soul you carry with you. Now, you can kiss me before you leave.

SEAN: We can't leave now.

MOTHER: You are to leave now. With Will. He'll take you to Cork and you will set sail for America.

ANNIE kisses her mother and buries her face in her shoulder.

Look after your brother, Annie.

ANNIE hugs her MOTHER even more tightly. SEAN gently prises them apart.

And I give you permission to insist that Sean washes his neck.

They laugh a little.

ANNIE: Mother?

MOTHER: Yes, my darling.

ANNIE: Where is 'Merica anyway?

*   *   *

A sudden blast of sea-air. Cork. The bustle of the docks, the curses of sailors, the screeching of gulls.

WILL: She's making ready to sail. The tide's in her favour. But we'll make it.

They run to the gangplank – CAPTAIN MURRAY stands at the top. He appears to be charm itself. A surly looking First Officer, MR BLUNDELL, stands by his side.

Captain! I want the best quarters you have for my two young friends. I want two berths on the upper deck and I want these children looked after like royalty.

CAPTAIN: I have a full ship, Sergeant. But I might find the room.

WILL: Captain, I'll pay you twenty pounds –

CAPTAIN: *(Disingenuous.)* Oh no, Sergeant, it is too much.

WILL: Each. As a seal of honour. But on the strict understanding that they travel in comfort. Under no circumstances will they travel in steerage.

He counts out the money and proffers it to the CAPTAIN.

Do I have your promise, Captain?

CAPTAIN: I am an officer and a gentleman. I will keep them under my personal supervision – they will be cared for as if they were my own.

WILL: They are in your charge. *(To SEAN, ANNIE.)* Here. Take my water bottle. And make sure it's filled afresh each day.

SEAN: Thank you.

WILL: Sean, Annie: you're on your own.

SEAN: Will you not come with us?

WILL: It's a voyage you must make yourselves. My direction is elsewhere.

And he descends the gangplank.

SEAN: Will you not be saying a proper goodbye, Will?

WILL walks on.

SEAN: Will you not be waving?

WILL: *(Without turning.)* Never look back, Sean. Never look back.

He disappears in the throng.

SEAN: *(To ANNIE.)* Let's go to the front of the ship and see if we can see America.

They proceed to the prow of the ship.

ANNIE: Will we not see Will again?

SEAN: No, I don't suppose we shall.

ANNIE: Nor Ireland?

SEAN: No. But we're going to America, Annie. We're going to find Father. He'll have bought a farm – 'tis hundreds of years since the O'Briens owned the land they worked on.

ANNIE: I can't see it.

SEAN: Can't see what?

ANNIE: 'Merica.

SEAN: Well, it's out there somewhere.

*　　*　　*

The ship's bell rings.

MR BLUNDELL: All hands on deck!

And 'All hands on deck!' is echoed throughout the ship.

CAPTAIN: My name is Captain Murray, late of Her Majesty's Royal Navy and Captain of this good ship *The Pelican*. I keep a tight ship, and expect you all to keep to the rules. If you abide by these rules, then I will treat you fairly – if not, well, it is for the good of the many that the few shall be reprimanded. We set a fair sail West on a brisk wind and true tide. My ship is your home; my home, your ship. You are the pioneers. I am your deliverer. May God bless you, *The Pelican*, and all who set sail in her for a New World!

Cheers to the echo at his rousing speech.

ANNIE: Mister Captain?

CAPTAIN: Yes, little lady?

ANNIE: I'm not little. Can you be telling me where we sleep, sir?

CAPTAIN: You'll be the Sergeant of Dragoons' girl. You'll accompany my First Officer, Mr Blundell here. He will show you where you will reside for the voyage.

ANNIE: Thank you, Captain.

CAPTAIN: And, young lady: I see you have about you something that is precious.

ANNIE clasps her neck in a vain attempt to hide the torc.

And if *I* have seen it, you can be certain that others on board will have spied it too. Beware of vagabonds, tinkers… Well, you know your fellow countrymen.

SEAN: Sir?

CAPTAIN: Mr Blundell.

MR BLUNDELL: Captain.

CAPTAIN: Be so kind as to lock away the young lady's valuables in my private quarters, for safe-keeping.

ANNIE: Sean? Do you think it wise?

SEAN: *(Unsure.)* I do, Annie. The Captain is right. 'Tis mixed company we keep aboard this ship. He will protect us and our torc.

ANNIE: *(To the CAPTAIN.)* Thank you, sir.

CAPTAIN: Please, it is my humble duty. Now, Mr Blundell, show them the comfort for which the Sergeant has so handsomely paid.

MR BLUNDELL: Ay, ay, Captain.

They descend into steerage. Around them in the gloom, they are aware of the creaking timbers, of wailing babies, retching bodies.

MR BLUNDELL: Make yourself a bed anywhere you can, anyhow you like. *(To SEAN.)* And report to me at dawn, young lad.

MR BLUNDELL leaves. ANNIE and SEAN proceed through the misery.

ANNIE: Why are they so sick, Sean?

EMIGRANT: 'Tis the malady of the sea. It will pass.

ANNIE: Is this the passage Will has paid for? Are these the quarters the Captain promised?

A shaft of radiant light picks out a FIDDLE PLAYER who starts to play a jig: feet tap; hands clap, and all are comforted by the music. When the fiddling has stopped, SEAN and ANNIE approach the FIDDLE PLAYER.

FIDDLE PLAYER: I'm as thin as a rake, so why don't you twos join me on the comfortable floor here. Very snug. There's not enough room to swing a mouse, is there, let alone –

SEAN/ANNIE: A ship's cat!

FIDDLE PLAYER/DONNELLY: *(Smiling at their quick-wit.)* My name is Liam Donnelly – I'm from County Sligo and Boston-bound like all these good folk here. There's not a lot I can do besides play my fiddle, but I'm mighty good at that, best in all Sligo, though I say it myself. I'm a modest sort of fellow, ain't I? And who might you be?

ANNIE: I'm Annie O'Brien, and he's my brother, Sean; and I'm hungry.

DONNELLY: Well, we'll not be having a feast here by the looks of it. But I've half a loaf of bread – all I have in the world, besides my fiddle. But my fiddle you can not eat. So, Annie O'Brien, you're welcome to share my bread. We've best be quiet about it though, for there's some hungry mouths around here and I've not enough for the feeding of the five thousand.

They eat the bread – he plays his fiddle: a gentle tune. SEAN offers him their water bottle.

Thank you. Now if I'm not mistaken – and I'm not often mistaken – you'll be the two the Captain has taken a shining to, will you not? Looking after you, is he?

ANNIE: Yes and he has our –

ANNIE is about to tell DONNELLY the whole story about the torc, but SEAN interrupts.

SEAN: To be sure.

DONNELLY: And what might he have, now?

SEAN: He has our best interests at heart, 'tis no more than that. I've to be up at first light to report to Mr Blundell. But don't tell the others, or they'll be as jealous as dogs.

Beat.

DONNELLY: Is that what it was? Well, let's talk no more about it. Here hold this.

He hands SEAN his fiddle.

Now, can you by any chance play the violin, Sean O'Brien?

SEAN: What's a vi-o-lin?

DONNELLY: *(Laughing.)* It's the fiddle you're holding in your hands.

SEAN: Oh, a fiddle! Yes, of course! Well, no. I don't know how to play it.

DONNELLY: Then you shall learn, for I shall teach you.

SEAN: But you make it sound so joyful.

DONNELLY: It's what's in your heart that makes it sing, Sean – ain't that right, Annie O'Brien?

ANNIE: I haven't an inkling of your meaning.

DONNELLY: When I reach Boston that's how I shall make my living.

SEAN: How?

DONNELLY: Teaching fiddle to every American who wants to learn. I know every Irish tune that has ever been written, or played – or has yet to be thought of. It would be a privilege and a pleasure, Sean O'Brien, for me to teach you. And it would assist my prospects greatly if I could be practising my teaching on you during the voyage.

SEAN: Why thank you.

DONNELLY: 'Tis nothing. If I can teach someone as ignorant as you, then it will be good practice for the Americans!

ANNIE: And what about me, Mister Fiddler? Can I not learn too?

DONNELLY: Certainly not, young Annie O'Brien.

ANNIE: And why not?

DONNELLY: Sure we've only the one fiddle between the three of us. So instead, I shall teach you to dance.

ANNIE: Why?

DONNELLY: Because your toes twinkle!

ANNIE: We have no money to pay for lessons, Mister.

DONNELLY: Nor I none to pay you.

ANNIE: Are you travelling on your own, Mister Fiddler?

DONNELLY: Not any more! Not any more.

He plays another jig and ANNIE dances – everyone stomps – this segues into...

*   *   *

SEAN on deck, scrubbing the timbers. The CAPTAIN and MR BLUNDELL watch.

SEAN: Captain.

CAPTAIN: Yes, my lad.

SEAN: Captain: are you sure we should be cooped up below in steerage? Didn't you give your word to Sergeant Will?

CAPTAIN: You may find it a little crowded on board to start with. Each time I head off with twice the cargo the ship can carry, but I know that 'natural wastage' will sadly ensure that half will never reach Boston. It used to be the same in the days of slaving. We take on board the many to the profit of the few.

He proceeds to his cabin.

SEAN: Is our torc safe, Mr Blundell? Is the Captain true to his word?

MR BLUNDELL: I've something on my mind I want to share with you.

SEAN: Mr Blundell?

SEAN looks up at him.

MR BLUNDELL: I know the torc rightly belongs to you and your sister. But now's not the time to trouble the Captain about the torc, Sean. Gold turns a good man rotten.

SEAN: I don't know if I follow your meaning.

MR BLUNDELL: You're a bright lad. You're ahead of the tide.

SEAN: *(Penny dropping.)* Mr Blundell: we have had that torc for over one thousand years. I'll not be the O'Brien who loses it.

MR BLUNDELL: Take my advice: you keep out of the Captain's eye-reach. He can be a monster when he's roused.

SEAN: The Captain?

MR BLUNDELL: It's this ship, this damned, rotten hulk of a ship and its rotten trade. It can twist your soul.

And this segues back to…

* * *

Below decks. DONNELLY and ANNIE and SEAN are having a fiddle/ dance lesson.

ANNIE: It's all my fault, Sean. Mother said to keep it hidden – and I plain forgot.

DONNELLY: Whatever it is you have lost, you must get it back. 'Tis too precious a thing for you to lose.

ANNIE: We didn't lose it; the Captain took it.

DONNELLY: And the Captain is a rogue.

ANNIE and SEAN look at each other, bruised.

He'll have it under lock and key.

SEAN: So how will we get it back?

ANNIE: Steal the key!

DONNELLY: No. Too dangerous.

ANNIE: Then it's hopeless.

DONNELLY: You cannot go in there and knock the Captain over the head and pinch his key, can you now?

ANNIE: Can't we?

DONNELLY: And even if you did manage to pick the lock, where would you hide it once you'd retrieved it? Mr Blundell would know who's taken it and then it'll be worse than scrubbing decks you'll be doing, Sean.

SEAN: So what do we do?

DONNELLY: Nothing.

SEAN: Nothing?

DONNELLY: The safest place to leave it for the moment is with the Captain. It can't walk away all by itself, can it now? Whatever it is that he's got of yours.

And he plays the fiddle, which segues into…

*　　*　　*

The CAPTAIN's cabin. A chest is open with the lock hacked off. MR BLUNDELL has SEAN by the collar while the CAPTAIN rants.

CAPTAIN: You, boy: I'll rope's-end you till you drop, you tinkering thief! Where have you hidden it?

SEAN: Hidden what?

CAPTAIN: Don't give me your feigned air of puzzlement, boy! Where have you hidden the necklet?

SEAN: Necklet?

CAPTAIN: Necklet, necklace – the gold, you tinker!

SEAN: I am *not* a tinker!

CAPTAIN: A wild Irish tinker that needs taming! I've yet to meet an Irishman who has not the morals of a rat. Now, hand it over!

SEAN: *(Enraged.)* The torc is ours! It belongs to our family. The O'Briens have had it for hundreds of years.

CAPTAIN: Which is why you have stolen it from me!

SEAN: I did not steal it!

CAPTAIN: You people. You have such minds, such imaginings. You are the bottom of the pile, the sweepings of the world, and yet you seem to believe that everyone else around you is a fool. I am not a fool, tinker boy. You came on board my ship barefoot, dressed in nothing but rags, and you claim the fine gold necklet that your scruffy sister was wearing was your own?! I will have you thrown in irons, I will clap you in chains.

SEAN: No. No!

CAPTAIN: Give me the necklet and I'll spare you the irons.

MR BLUNDELL: Do as the Captain says.

SEAN looks at MR BLUNDELL ganging up on him.

SEAN: *(To the CAPTAIN.)* I've done nothing, sir!

CAPTAIN: Then we will have to beat it out of you. Mr Blundell.

MR BLUNDELL: Captain Murray: if we flog him, sir, it might set the other passengers into revolt. Better to send him up the crow's nest. A night aloft in this ocean will change his mind: the freezing wind will loosen his tongue.

The CAPTAIN hesitates. SEAN is devastated at this betrayal by MR BLUNDELL.

CAPTAIN: He doesn't come down until he confesses.

MR BLUNDELL grabs SEAN by the scruff of the neck and manhandles him to the rigging. Nonetheless he speaks gently to SEAN.

MR BLUNDELL: You'll be all right. It's better than a flogging or a week in chains. Just don't look down; and see that you have a good grip with both your hands before you move your legs.

SEAN: But where's the torc? Have *you* stolen it?

MR BLUNDELL: Take this – *(He hands him a small flask.)* – it'll keep the cold out.

SEAN climbs aloft into the night sky. The mast swings sickeningly – he slips, but manages to pull himself into the holed water barrel that is the precarious crow's nest. He drinks a tot of the liquid – and spits it out. Rum. He takes another sip, swallows, winces – and then smiles as it puts fire in his belly. He sings the songs DONNELLY has taught him, to keep his spirits up.

*   *   *

Time passes and dawn breaks, golden and crimson on the horizon. SEAN peers ahead – and then his mouth drops and his excitement explodes.

SEAN: *(Bellowing.)* Land! I see land! I see America!

ALL clamber on deck below, the CAPTAIN spies the land through his telescope.

CAPTAIN: I have it! A perfect landfall.

SEAN then sees a darkening cloud on the horizon.

SEAN: Storm-cloud! I see a storm brewing!

CAPTAIN: What do you mean, boy? The sky is beautiful.

MR BLUNDELL: The sky over there may look pretty, but it's as vicious a sky as I've ever seen. It won't be long before the storm hits us – we'll need the boy down here to man the pumps.

The CAPTAIN hesitates.

CAPTAIN: You're not to leave him out of your sight.

MR BLUNDELL: Ay, ay, Captain.

The storm brews.

(Bellowing, to SEAN.) Descend the mast! Descend the mast! *(To the crew.)* Haul in the mainsail! Batten down all hatches! We may have America in sight, but there'll be one hell of a storm before we reach her!

But there's a sudden lull and stillness – they all pause in the momentary calm before the storm.

It's on its way. Won't be long now.

And sure enough, the storm hits and all hell breaks loose – SEAN struggles as he makes the perilous descent from the crow's nest. The top-mast comes down with a yawning crash. As SEAN reaches the deck, MR BLUNDELL cries out to him.

Go to your sister! We shall go on the rocks. When she strikes, stay below until she settles.

SEAN: Below decks? We'll drown!

MR BLUNDELL: You'll never survive if you're thrown overboard into the sea. Get below and stay there!

SEAN does as he's told. Pandemonium below decks. ANNIE comes running to him.

ANNIE: Sean! Sean! Where is it? Where's the torc?

DONNELLY comes running too.

DONNELLY: Here. Take my fiddle. If anything should happen to me, you're to have it.

SEAN: But what about the torc? Mr Blundell has betrayed us.

DONNELLY: The torc is your talisman. It will keep you safe.

And he runs out on deck, leaving them with the fiddle case.

ANNIE: Quick, Sean. Let's follow!

SEAN: No, Mr Blundell said to wait below decks.

ANNIE: What?!

SEAN: It's our only chance.

ANNIE: And you trust him?

There's another crash from above.

SEAN: They've no hope up there. No hope at all. All storms must end sometime. If the ship doesn't break up, we'll have a chance.

And there's an almighty climax where it sounds as if the ship has indeed broken up catastrophically –

Blackout.

Pause.

*　　*　　*

Calm after the storm.

The lights rise. SEAN and ANNIE wade through the flotsam of death to the shore, clutching DONNELLY's fiddle case.

SEAN: Mr Blundell! Fiddler Donnelly?

Only the gulls reply.

ANNIE: Is this 'Merica? Do you think it's really 'Merica?

SEAN: 'Spose it must be.

ANNIE: Are we alone?

SEAN looks around him.

SEAN: Yes.

ANNIE: Why do we always leave everyone behind? Why does everyone we love have to leave us?

SEAN: Donnelly left us his fiddle. Said we should play it and dance to it – and we will. And whenever we do, we shall remember him.

He opens the case and takes out the fiddle. It rattles. He shakes it: it rattles some more. He looks inside the fiddle.

ANNIE: What is it Sean?

SEAN: 'Tis the torc. 'Tis the golden torc. The two of them hid it for us, Annie: Mr Blundell and Fiddler Donnelly.

ANNIE: And we'll never be able to thank them.

They let this thought sink in.

I'm so hungry, I could eat a horse.

SEAN: Then let's find one!

They walk along the beach.

ANNIE: 'Merica is quite different from Ireland.

SEAN: Do you think?

ANNIE: Well look: more trees grow here than I've ever seen in my life. And they're all great tall trees – not bent and stunted by the wind like back home. And the leaves shine scarlet and gold.

Some of the leaves fall like snowflakes around them.

Beautiful.

They hear a rustling in the leaves.

Listen. Did you hear that?

The rustling gets louder.

SEAN: *(To the rustling.)* It's only us: Sean and Annie O'Brien! Who's there?

More rustling.

We're from the ship. Who are you?

And a PIG lets out an almighty squeal which frightens the living daylights out of SEAN and ANNIE before it goes grunting off.

ANNIE: *(Laughing.)* 'Tis a pig, a 'Merican pig! And you were so scared!

SEAN: Wasn't.

ANNIE: Yes you was.

SEAN: So were you. Let's follow it.

ANNIE: Why?

SEAN: Because if it's anything like an Irish pig, its nose will be taking it home. And its home will be a farm. And a farm will have food. And people.

*   *   *

They follow it and come to a village – where dogs yap at them.

ANNIE: How do we know they'll be friendly?

SEAN: We don't.

The hiss of geese and cackle of hens scattering. And then a group of VILLAGERS approach, one holding a gun. Both sides keep a wary distance.

ANNIE: Is this Boston, 'Merica?

A VILLAGER sniggers.

(Raising her voice and ar-ti-cu-la-ting slow-ly to foreigners) We Are Loo-king For Bos-ton, 'Me-ri-ca…

The VILLAGERS all laugh.

VILLAGER: Hell no! This ain't Boston! Boston's a mite bigger'n this.

The VILLAGERS laugh again.

VILLAGER: You gone and got yourself lost in them woods, I guess. Why, you ain't more'n little children!

ANNIE: We're *not little…*

VILLAGER: What's your ma and pa doing lettin' you run wild out in them woods? Where you from anyhow? You ain't from hereabouts.

SEAN: We come from Ireland. And the ship we were on went on the rocks in the storm.

The smiles vanish – the gun is raised.

VILLAGER: Ireland? You on one of them migrant ships?

SEAN: Yes.

VILLAGER: Did you have the sickness on board?

ANNIE: The malady of the sea, some of them had.

VILLAGER: I knew it! A plague ship. You keep your distance, do you hear? Don't come any closer.

The gun is cocked.

SEAN: What's the matter? Why are you looking at us like that?

VILLAGER: 'Cos you got the plague, that's why. Git back, else I'll shoot. And that's a promise.

SEAN: But we need food. And water. Won't you give us some water?

VILLAGER: You got any kin-folk, any family?

ANNIE: Of course we have! We've come to 'Merica to look for our father. Perhaps you know him? Patrick O'Brien's his name. Big fellow.

The VILLAGERS chuckle again.

SEAN: Can you tell us how far it is to Boston?

VILLAGER: Fifteen miles – twelve if you keep to the coast road.

The VILLAGERS confer in whispers.

ANNIE: Hey, what are you all whispering about?

VILLAGER: We're thinking it wouldn't be right for us to have you walking all the way to Boston on an empty stomach, not with night coming on and winter in the air.

SEAN: No.

VILLAGER: So here's what we're gonna do: we'll bring you what you need, and you kin go in with the fish wagon into Boston.

SEAN: That's very kind.

VILLAGER: Hell, yes! *(To themselves.)* Though you ain't smelled the fish wagon… *(To ANNIE/SEAN.)* Follow me.

*   *   *

They do, at a distance. The VILLAGERS bring a fresh set of clothes and two pairs of boots. Music plays under the following.

ANNIE and SEAN change into the clothes.

ANNIE: They're too big!

SEAN: But no holes. And they're warm. And dry.

ANNIE: How do you get these boots on? I don't think I've ever worn a pair of boots in my life.

SEAN: You squeeze 'em on with an oomph – and then stamp around. Just like Father.

They do so.

ANNIE: Sean, Sean, I feel like dancing!

SEAN gets out the fiddle and plays a jig, which ANNIE dances, lifting her new woollen skirt above her boots as she does so. The VILLAGERS gather.

VILLAGER: Where's you learn to play and dance like that?

ANNIE: We had a friend. He taught us. But he's dead now, so we'll be playing and dancing for him from now on.

VILLAGER: You take good care in Boston. 'S'a wicked town for young folk like you to be 'lone in.

VILLAGER: Good luck little people. Safe journey.

And they leap up onto the cart – driven by MARTY.

MARTY: You sits on the back thar and I'll not catch the plague – though judgin' by the way you dancin' little lady, if you have got the plague then I'd like it too!

ANNIE: Your wagon's a bit smelly.

MARTY: Aw, there are worse smells than fresh fish.

He chews tobacco and spits impressively.

SEAN: How do you do that?

MARTY: Thar's an art to it. Why, I kin knock a hairy-legged buzzard clean off his post at fifty paces. Don't kill him of course, but he hears it a-coming and he knows it's one of mine so he don't wait around, no sir.

ANNIE: Can I have a go?

SEAN: Annie!

MARTY: Why surely, ma'am. Chew on this leathery baccy until your jaw aches – then use your tongue like a catapult.

She does – spectacularly.

SEAN: How did you…?

ANNIE: Away she goes!

They spit their way to Boston.

*   *   *

Boston: a teeming city of refugees. Cold and grey and snowing.

SEAN: 'A Paradise aplenty where the sun's always shining…'? – not in Boston, not in winter.

40

ANNIE: Have you ever seen so many people? Sure 'tis teeming like an anthill.

MARTY: Well good luck. Here's half a dollar. And mind whom you talk to.

And he rides off.

ANNIE: How will we ever find Father?

BOSTON CHANCER: *(Smiling broadly.)* Have you just got in from the Old Country?

The CHILDREN nod.

And I suppose you'll be looking for somewhere to sleep? *(Not waiting for an answer.)* Well you've met the right fellow. I've a little attic room, just suit you fine. Two dollars a week – ain't that a bargain?

ANNIE: But we've only half a dollar.

SEAN looks daggers at ANNIE.

BOSTON CHANCER: All right, I'm a fair man. You're down on your luck, I can see that. A dollar and a half, how will that be?

SEAN: We're not looking for somewhere to stay, Mister.

BOSTON CHANCER: In this winter? You're kidding me! Now what about that fiddle? It must be worth a fair bit. I'll take it off you and you have the room for free for a fortnight.

SEAN: *(Gripping the case tightly to him.)* 'Tis not mine to sell.

BOSTON CHANCER: *(Advancing.)* Then I'll just borrow it for a while.

A tall BLACK MAN appears.

BLACK MAN: *(To BOSTON CHANCER.)* You after somethin' friend?

The BOSTON CHANCER weighs up the situation.

'Cos if you are, you gotta remember that these is my friends, an' if they don't like you then I don't either. Get my meanin', friend?

The BOSTON CHANCER scarpers.

Now you two is gonna get into all kinds of trouble. I's can see I's gonna have to keep my eye on you two.

ANNIE: But how do we know you are our friend?

BLACK MAN: Am I bein' *un*friendly? Hope that fiddle of yours ain't broke, boy.

SEAN opens the fiddle case, rattles the fiddle.

SEAN: Nothing broken.

BLACK MAN: You sure, boy? It rattles some, somethin' loose inside maybe?

SEAN: *(Slamming shut the lid of the case.)* No.

BLACK MAN: That there is a fine fiddle.

ANNIE: I'm Annie, and my brother's called Sean. We are O'Briens.

BLACK MAN/LIL' LUKE: An' I'm Lil' Luke, Miss Annie. My privilege, my privilege.

He raises his hat.

ANNIE: Why are you called Little Luke? You're not little, you're big. We had a brother called Little Joe. But he *was* little – the littlest.

LIL' LUKE: I was lil' when I was born, an' that's when my mammy first knew me, so I guess that's why she called me Lil' Luke, an' it's kinda stuck.

ANNIE: You speak very good English.

LIL' LUKE: I been speakin' it all my life, lil' missy.

ANNIE: Then can you tell us if you've seen our father, Mister Patrick O'Brien?

LIL' LUKE: When, missy?

ANNIE: Oh, about a year ago.

LIL' LUKE: Well if he were here that long ago, he sure ain't likely to be here now. If he got any sense he'll be long gone.

SEAN: Yes. Out West.

LIL' LUKE: Well that's where they all head for in the end.

ANNIE: How did you get so black, Mister?

SEAN: Annie!

LIL' LUKE: *(Chuckling.)* Well, I puts it on every morning before sun-up and I takes it off every night. You rub me hard enough and it'll come off just like the brown off a hen's egg. You wanna try?

He offers her his face – and she rubs it, but of course nothing happens.

(Mock shock-horror.) Well, bless my soul, looks as if I put it on once too often! Now I'm stuck with it for life.

He smiles. ANNIE realises he's been teasing her.

ANNIE: Are you telling me you were born like that?

LIL' LUKE: That's what my Mammy said. You mean you ain't never seen no black man before?

ANNIE: In Ireland everyone's white. Well, dirty white.

LIL' LUKE: And there was me thinking that you were all little green folk in Ireland!

ANNIE: Really?

LIL' LUKE raises an eyebrow as if to say 'what do you think?'

LIL' LUKE: We got all sorts here in 'Merica, folks from all over: England, Ireland, Dutchland, Swedenland. Hundreds of 'em comin' in every day. 'Cos this is a mighty big country an' there's room for everyone who's a mind to come. *(To SEAN.)* You play that fiddle of yours?

SEAN: *(Clutching the fiddle case tightly to him.)* A bit.

LIL' LUKE: Yes you keep a tight hold of it. But if you play, you may be able to earn yourself a crust. So long. I must get back to my ladies. Take care now, d'you hear?

He leaves. Snow falls. The chill wind whines.

ANNIE: What did he mean, his 'ladies'? What did he mean, 'earn ourselves a crust'?

SEAN: I guess he means that we could play for money. I could play. You could dance.

ANNIE: *(Affronted.)* I won't beg!

SEAN: 'Tis not exactly begging. And we'll need the money to get us to Father.

ANNIE: You think he's still…

She means 'alive'; SEAN knows what she means.

SEAN: Yes, Annie. And we must deliver him the torc. It's our talisman. Our family charm. And that's why we're going to stand on this street corner and I'm going to play the fiddle and they'll throw money into the fiddle case as they pass by, enough to keep us in food, and enough to pay the rent on some little room somewhere, enough to keep us going until we can find out where Father's gone. Now that's not begging, is it Annie? That's working for a living.

ANNIE: S'pose.

SEAN: And you're going to dance, Annie. You're going to dance as you've never danced before.

SEAN plays; ANNIE dances; PASSERSBY throw money into the fiddle case. The snow snows. The freezing wind blows. They play and dance on, determined. Eventually it is too much and ANNIE collapses. A CROWD gathers. A LADY IN BLUE pushes forward.

LADY IN BLUE: Stand aside! Stand aside!

She looks down at a distraught SEAN cradling an unconscious ANNIE in his arms.

We should be ashamed to see such a sight on our city streets. Christmas Eve is it not? And was there not another child somewhere else who could find no shelter on just such an evening? Are we nothing but innkeepers that we stand gaping and do nothing? Little Luke! Pick up that child and bring her with us this instant.

LIL' LUKE: Yes, Ma'am.

LIL' LUKE steps forward and takes ANNIE from SEAN.

BYSTANDER: But Ma'am, the child could be dying of the plague!

LADY IN BLUE: Tell me, Sir, are you a doctor?

BYSTANDER: No, Ma'am.

LADY IN BLUE: Then, Sir, you have no right to make a medical judgement on the matter, have you?

BYSTANDER: No, Ma'am.

LADY IN BLUE: Quite so. And even if the child had been touched by the plague, every member of my family has lived out their three-score years and ten, and I shall do the same, plague or no plague.

BYSTANDER: Three-score years and ten is quite sufficient for anyone, Ma'am.

LADY IN BLUE: *(Looking daggers at him.)* One must not be greedy, Sir.

BYSTANDER: No, Ma'am.

LADY IN BLUE: And Luke, you'd better bring that wretched boy too. *(To her SISTER.)* I have never liked boys, Martha, as you know.

MISS MARTHA: No, Henry.

LADY IN BLUE/MISS HENRY: Such unnecessary creatures, boys. But if we take the one then I suppose we shall have to take the other.

MISS MARTHA: Yes, Henry.

SEAN: *(Through his tears to LIL' LUKE.)* My sister: is she dead?

LIL' LUKE: Hard to tell, Sean O'Brien, hard to tell.

MISS HENRY: As soon as we get some warm food into her, and tuck her up in a nice warm bed, she'll be living and breathing again.

SEAN: Thank you, Ma'am!

They set off, LIL' LUKE carrying ANNIE in his arms.

MISS HENRY: Don't thank me. Thank Little Luke. Thank my sister, Martha.

MISS MARTHA: Oh, you're being too modest, Henry. Since we first saw those poor wretches from Ireland pouring off the ships, you said we should try to help them if we could.

MISS HENRY: But there are too many of them. The problem is too big.

MISS MARTHA: Which is why we are helping those that we can, Henry.

SEAN: Why does your sister call you Henry? You're not a man, you're a lady.

MISS HENRY: Well, young man, I am a lady, always have been. But our mother found it difficult to tell us apart, so she cut off all my hair and called me Henry, and let Martha's grow long and called her…Martha. Ah, home.

They stop in front of a gabled, red-brick mansion, bristling with smoking chimneys.

ANNIE: So many chimneys!

SEAN: *(Overwhelmed that ANNIE has revived.)* Annie!

ANNIE: Why do you need more than one?

MISS HENRY: Well, one would be lonely.

ANNIE: Father built the tallest chimney in Ireland – and he's going to build the tallest in 'Merica too.

MISS MARTHA: You have a father, then? Here in America?

ANNIE: To be sure we have. But we don't know where in 'Merica.

SEAN: Out West, maybe.

MISS MARTHA: And your mother?

ANNIE looks at SEAN.

SEAN: She's dead, Miss Martha.

ANNIE: Yes. She's dead.

Their eyes fill with tears.

MISS HENRY: Well come along now. Up to the bathroom with you. There's enough dirt on your neck young man to grow a whole field of potatoes!

They run off, LIL' LUKE following. MISS MARTHA and MISS HENRY watch them go.

MISS MARTHA: Poor sweet children. We are their refuge, Henry.

MISS HENRY: And we shall keep them as long as they need us.

MISS MARTHA: You've a heart of gold under all that bluster.

MISS HENRY: Hm. Now we have them here we shall educate them. Can you imagine what kind of life they must have had, Martha? And they'll no longer need to go busking in the streets.

MISS MARTHA: Their violin is precious to them – that young man clutches it to him as if it were a part of him.

MISS HENRY: It is. It is in his blood. Without it they would have perished in the streets of Boston, like so many others.

MISS MARTHA: We shall give them a Christmas they will never forget.

*   *   *

We segue into SEAN and ANNIE delighting the assembled COMPANY with their spirited Christmas playing and dancing – SEAN spruced up in waistcoat, ANNIE in a clean white dress, wearing the golden torc, and stomping in her boots. Christmas decorations festooned throughout.

LIL' LUKE: *(To MISS MARTHA.)* There's something about those lil' children. They bring happiness wherever they go. Why just look at Miss Henry: have you ever seen her dancin' before?

She is dancing.

MISS MARTHA: Not since we were children ourselves.

LIL' LUKE: An' she's laughin' too! Don't she usually sit by the fire at Christmas glowerin' and wishin' everyone'd go home? Jus' look at her now!

MISS HENRY: *(Dancing, to SEAN.)* Faster, young man! Faster!

ANNIE: Miss Henry: this is the best day of my life!

MISS HENRY: And you look so pretty. Your necklace is beautiful.

SEAN stops his playing.

SEAN: I told you not to wear it, Annie.

MISS HENRY: Why, child?

SEAN: It is the torc of the O'Briens. One thousand years old. From when we owned great lands and forests all of our own. Wherever we O'Briens go, this torc goes with us. It protects us from danger. It is the O'Brien soul we carry with us. It has preserved us – and destroys all those who steal it. So long as we keep the torc, then the O'Briens will never die out. It is our secret. And now you share our secret.

MISS HENRY: To be trusted with such a secret is an honour, young man.

ANNIE: You are the nicest, kindest, goodest people we know.

MISS HENRY: Goodest?

MISS MARTHA: Let it pass, Henry. Now children, you must go to bed.

ANNIE: I could stay here for ever.

MISS MARTHA: And so you shall, Annie dear, if you care to.

SEAN: But we can't. Or we'll never see Father again.

MISS HENRY: Of course. And that you must do. We will help you find him.

*   *   *

It's night time – and the house is still and silent: the breathing and gentle snoring of SLEEPERS. SEAN and ANNIE tiptoe along the corridor.

ANNIE: *(Whispering.)* But it's so ungrateful!

SEAN: *(Whispering.)* If we're going, then it's best to go now while everyone's asleep. We can't look them in the face and say we're going, not after all their kindnesses. I couldn't bear to see the hurt in their eyes.

They carry on creeping along the corridor – and bump into LIL' LUKE.

LIL' LUKE: *(Whispering.)* Miss Martha and Miss Henry said you might be goin'. They told me you weren't to go without havin' breakfast first. They's waitin' for you in the parlour.

They walk sheepishly into the dimly lit parlour where MISS MARTHA and MISS HENRY await.

MISS HENRY: Headin' West?

SEAN nods.

The wagon trains roll further West each year, but there's a lot of plain and prairie and desert to cross before you reach that other ocean all that way from ours. Takes a year or more to get there.

SEAN: A year?

MISS HENRY: It is three thousand miles across a wild continent peopled with wild and wicked men and marauding savages. Your father may well have made it. But many a thing can happen to a man between Boston and California.

SEAN: But we have to try.

MISS MARTHA: We know you do, Sean. But you will need a wagon and provisions, and someone to take you as far as the big river.

ANNIE: The big river?

MISS MARTHA: Yes. There you will find our brother, the Colonel.

ANNIE: We didn't know you had a brother.

MISS HENRY: No. Well, Miss Martha and I prefer to forget. Our father left us a great fortune, from his furniture business here in Boston. Miss Martha and I invested our share wisely; but our brother had other ideas. He was a soldier of fortune, fought the English, the Mexicans, the Red Indians…well, now he has a ship of iniquity on the Ohio River.

ANNIE: What's the O-hi-o-high-river? What is a ship of ink-willity?

MISS HENRY: Never you mind. Little Luke: you know you are a free man – have been since the day you escaped from slavery in the Deep South, all those years ago. So you do not have to do what I'm about to ask you –

LITTLE LUKE: No need to ask, Miss Henry; it's the best an' only way for these children to find their Papa. I's already on my way.

MISS HENRY: The Colonel will be moored at Wheeling, Ohio. Hand them over into his safe-keeping. He'll then sail them up the Missouri river to St Louis.

LIL' LUKE: I surely will, Miss Henry. And I'll return here by the Fall.

MISS MARTHA: And you can return here one day too children. This will always be your home.

SEAN: Thank you, Miss Martha.

MISS HENRY: Now get along. I've packed blankets and clothes and enough provisions to keep you going for a month or so.

ANNIE: Thank you, Miss Henry. *(She gives MISS HENRY a big hug.)*

MISS HENRY: *(Tearful.)* Now you've set me going. Be off!

MISS MARTHA: But take this – *(She presents them with a gleaming black revolver.)* – it was our father's. Just in case you should ever need it. It would only rust back here in Boston.

MISS HENRY: And here's a letter to my despicable brother: I have never asked anything of him, and it appeals to his better nature – if he's still got one.

ANNIE: Thank you Miss Henry, Miss Martha. We shall never forget you.

MISS HENRY: Oh you'll meet other kind people on your way and if…and *when* you make it to California, Miss Martha and I will be long gone.

MISS HENRY and MISS MARTHA leave.

ANNIE: Lil' Luke: is it far to Wheeling, O-hi-o-high-o?

LIL' LUKE: I don' know 'cos I ain't never bin there.

SEAN: But you do know where you're going?

LIL' LUKE: All the way down through Pennsylvania. Close to a thousand miles I reckon.

SEAN: A thousand miles!

LIL' LUKE: So we'd better get goin'.

* * *

They set off in the wagon.

ANNIE: We won't see them again, Sean, will we?

SEAN doesn't answer.

Why did Miss Martha give us her father's gun?

LIL' LUKE: If you goes on askin' questions all the way, you'll talk yo'self dumb before you git there.

SEAN: I've never ever fired a gun.

LIL' LUKE: Well let's hope you never have to. I'm gonna teach you how to lasso, and how to trap a rattlesnake safely, how to light a fire with damp twigs –

ANNIE: I know how to do that already – I'm from Ireland, remember.

LIL' LUKE: Now I'm feelin' kinda sad myself, leaving Miss Martha and Miss Henry behind, so why don't you git out your fiddle Master Sean and we can sing sumpin' to cheer our spirits. 'Sgonna be a long, hard road.

And they sing a Spiritual, and play the fiddle, and tap their feet, as they travel on their way as Winter turns to Spring, and…

Interval.

PART II

America. Spring 1848.

LIL' LUKE, SEAN and ANNIE set up camp. Music dies away…

ANNIE: Why can't we come hunting with you?

LIL' LUKE: One person's got jus' two feet; two persons' got four; and three's –

ANNIE: Got six!

LIL' LUKE: Three persons always smell thrice as bad to a critter. You get the fire goin'.

He goes off. The cicadas chirr. The flies buzz.

SEAN: We should get the fire going like Lil' Luke says. These flies'll eat us alive if we don't smoke 'em out.

ANNIE: Sure they're not as bad as the midges back home.

SEAN: Maybe they's all partial to Irish blood the world over? There's not a bit of me they haven't eaten.

ANNIE is looking off into the trees, worried.

Is something the matter, Annie?

ANNIE: The trees: they moved.

SEAN: Don't be daft. 'Tis just the wind.

ANNIE: *(Whispering.)* But I think someone's looking at us.

He goes towards the trees and peers into them.

SEAN: No. No one. It's the wind and the noises it makes. Sounds will carry along a valley, you know. 'Tis nothing, Annie.

LIL' LUKE returns with a rabbit.

And here is Lil' Luke. It was him all along.

LIL' LUKE: What was me? And why haven't you got the fire goin'?

SEAN: Annie thought she heard things in the trees.

ANNIE: And saw them moving too.

LIL' LUKE: There's nobody here but ourselves.

ANNIE sees something move again.

ANNIE: There!

They all look in that direction – and as they do so, a BOUNTY HUNTER dressed in shredded leather jerkin and wide-brimmed hat enters behind them, rifle at the ready.

BOUNTY HUNTER: Nice an' easy.

They freeze.

I don't want to hurt no one. Not 'less I have to.

LIL' LUKE: Miss Annie, Sean, you stay right by me. This man won't hurt us none. He just wanna take our things. That's all. And things ain't that important, not 'nough to git killed for anyhow. Anyways, he won't find nothin' in that ole wagon 'cos we ain't got nothin', 'cept a few blankets.

BOUNTY HUNTER: That's where you're wrong – now I'm gonna have a little look through your wagon, 'case there's somethin' worth havin' in there. And I sure as hell could do with a-eatin' of your rabbit there. But it's *you* I'm after. *(To LIL' LUKE.)* I trade in men like you. Bounty Hunter they calls me. I comes up north every spring, catches me a fine crop of runaway slaves and I sells them down south. All I gotta do is git you down into Kentucky and there's folk there'll pay me more'n fifty dollars apiece for runaways. Better trade than horse thievin' – 'cos it's legal an' you don't git hung for it. They got cotton down there an' they ain't 'nough people to pick it, so I's takin' you back home.

LIL' LUKE: I'm a free man – bin free for thirty years or more.

BOUNTY HUNTER: You's a slave, you all are, don't you know that yet? You born a slave, you die a slave. Now you kin die right here if you've a mind to, or you kin ride out with me nice and easy.

ANNIE: Don't go, Little Luke, don't go!

LIL' LUKE: Miss Annie, the man's got a rifle. There ain't nothin' I kin do; and, what's more, there ain't nothin' you kin do.

SEAN: *(To BOUNTY HUNTER.)* Mister: if we were to have something maybe worth fifty dollars or more, would you take that instead of Little Luke?

BOUNTY HUNTER: 'Pends on what you got, son.

LIL' LUKE: *(To SEAN.)* Don't bargain with the devil, Master Sean; don't do it.

SEAN: *(Ignoring him.)* 'Tis gold, mister. If I let you have it, will you let Little Luke go and leave us alone?

BOUNTY HUNTER: If it's worth more'n fifty dollars, son, then you got yourself a deal. But I gotta see it first.

SEAN: Shall I be fetching it then?

BOUNTY HUNTER: *(Motioning with his rifle.)* Let the little girl do it.

ANNIE, about to protest that she's not little, chooses to bite her lip.

SEAN: Fetch it, Annie.

ANNIE goes to fetch the fiddle case – taking her time, stuffing something else down her shirt.

Have you got it, Annie?

ANNIE: Got it.

She returns with the fiddle case.

BOUNTY HUNTER: So it's a fiddle, a golden fiddle! Stop wasting my time.

SEAN: Open it, Annie. Take it out and show him.

She takes out the golden torc – it dazzles the BOUNTY HUNTER, but then he snatches it from ANNIE, and bites it – as he does so, ANNIE whips the revolver out from beneath her shirt and points it at the BOUNTY HUNTER.

ANNIE: Mister: you drop that rifle and throw down the torc, else I'll shoot you, mister, I will, I'll shoot you.

A Mexican stand-off. Then the BOUNTY HUNTER chuckles.

Don't you be laughing at me, mister…

BOUNTY HUNTER: You forgotten to cock it, little lady.

And he simply reaches forward and takes the revolver out of her trembling hands.

BOUNTY HUNTER: *(To SEAN.)* Now you tie the slave's hands behind his back.

SEAN does as he's told.

SEAN: What'll you do with little Luke?

BOUNTY HUNTER: Don't you worry none; I'll take real good care of him. He's worth more to me 'live than dead – but even 'live he ain't worth the gold in this necklace of your'n. There's enough gold here to buy ten a' him. So I'll be thankin' you for the gold as well, an' I'll be on my way. I'm much obliged, my friends; mighty obliged. Be seein' you.

And the BOUNTY HUNTER leads LIL' LUKE off at the end of his rifle.

ANNIE: How was I to know you had to cock it first?

SEAN: Wouldn't have helped, Annie. It wasn't loaded anyway. Miss Martha forgot to give us the bullets.

ANNIE: So what'll we do?

SEAN: Well, we got the fiddle.

ANNIE: How will that help?

SEAN: Follow me.

She does.

* * *

LIL' LUKE is in shackles by a camp fire. The BOUNTY HUNTER dozes, rifle in hand. The wind rustles the bushes – and an eerie whining wafts on the breeze. The BOUNTY HUNTER awakes.

BOUNTY HUNTER: You hear that?

LIL' LUKE: Cain't hear nuttin'.

The whine whines again.

BOUNTY HUNTER: You deaf, or sumpin'?

LIL' LUKE: No, I hear that, and I'm afraid, mighty afraid.

BOUNTY HUNTER: What?

LIL' LUKE: Ain't you heard about the Injuns and their summonin' up o'their ancestors' spirits?

BOUNTY HUNTER: Hogwash!

LIL' LUKE: Hogwash or not, I'm sure as I'm livin' that that is a sound of somethin' mighty fierce. An' I don't want to lose my scalp.

The scraping whining comes closer – the BOUNTY HUNTER is scared.

It's a' comin' for us! It's a' comin' for us!

And just as the whining reaches an excruciating climax – the BOUNTY HUNTER runs off, terrified.

You ain't foolin' me, chillun'. I's heard you practising that fiddle enough to know you can make it squeak and scare the fleas off the back of a cat. Now untie me quick and let's get outa here.

ANNIE rushes on – SEAN keeps lookout – and unties LIL' LUKE and then they all scarper.

Then LIL' LUKE gives ANNIE and SEAN a kiss.

SEAN: Hey! What's that for?

LIL' LUKE: I ain't a kissin' kinda man, but I ain't got nuttin' else to thank you with. You saved my life.

ANNIE: 'Twas nothing.

LIL' LUKE: You kin drive horses, cook beans, play the fiddle, sing and dance like a princess and scare off bounty hunters without ever firin' a shot. Ain't nothin' gonna stop you children, nothin'.

ANNIE: But he has still got the torc. Without that, we have nothing.

LIL' LUKE: Well, we still have each other.

The sound of a river.

SEAN: What's that gushing noise?

LIL' LUKE: That's what we came for. That is the sound of the great Ohio river. And we's gonna find us the sisters' Colonel-brother.

ANNIE: Where should we look?

LIL' LUKE: In the nearest saloon bar on Main Street.

ANNIE: How d'you know he'll be there?

LIL' LUKE: 'Cos he's a drinker an' a gambler an' that's the only place he can be entertainin' such past-times. Now you wait here.

And LIL' LUKE enters a saloon bar – a thwackatackatack of the swing doors momentarily releasing the sound of male laughter, honky-tonk piano, breaking glasses – leaving the CHILDREN outside.

ANNIE: D'you think the Bounty Hunter will come this way too, looking for Little Luke?

SEAN: Not while he's got the torc.

ANNIE: D'you think he'll try to sell it?

SEAN: I'm afraid he will.

ANNIE: But it isn't his to sell!

SEAN: It's his to do with as he wants now, Annie.

The doors to the saloon bar open – thwackatackatack, laughter, honky-tonk piano – and a tall, ELEGANT MAN in grey suit stands there, leaning on his silver-topped cane.

ELEGANT MAN: I'm told I have to take you under my wing. But I'm not going to do what I'm told. If I do take you on, it will be because I want to. You will both accompany me to my riverboat. She awaits.

ANNIE: Who are you, mister?

ELEGANT MAN: I am the brother of your benefactresses.

ANNIE: The Colonel?

ELEGANT MAN/COLONEL: Follow me.

*   *   *

The three-tiered paddle-steamer sails into view – the paddle-wheels, the funnel.

COLONEL: I have considered what will be done, and you will not like any of it. First, I have sent Little Luke home to Boston. My sisters will be missing him and he's done all he can for you.

SEAN: But we never said goodbye!

ANNIE: Couldn't he have come with us?

COLONEL: It's dangerous for him out West, as you now, no doubt, appreciate. Second, I can offer little hope that you will recover your golden torc, as I believe you call it. There are many such scoundrels as this bounty hunter, wicked men who feed like vultures on the unwary and innocent. We'd be lucky to find his needle in that haystack. Thirdly, as for finding your father, I can be no more optimistic. I have seen many an Irishman pass through, heading West, but who knows if any of them were your father; and even if one of them was, who's to say he made it across the plains and desert? Finally, your journey to California

will take you longer than you imagine. You will have to
be patient. You will need to prepare before you set out
on the two thousand mile journey across the great plains
towards Oregon and California. You will rest aboard this
boat as she sails down river. I cannot pretend that I like the
arrangement, but what has to be done has to be done.

ANNIE: Hm. Firstly, we would have liked to say goodbye to
Little Luke, but we were once told to never look back.
Secondly, we'll find our torc, I know we will, Mister
Colonel. Thirdly, if you point us in the right direction, we'll
find Father too. And finally, why do you call this paddle-
steamer 'she'? Does she have a name?

COLONEL: She does. The *Henry Martha*, after my sisters.

ANNIE: Back in Boston, your sister Miss Henry said you were
'spicable, whatever that might mean. Why did she you call
you 'spicable?

COLONEL: Annie O'Brien: if I was to ask you to tell me the
wickedest thing you had ever done, would you tell me?

ANNIE: Yes.

COLONEL: Well you tell me and then I'll tell you.

ANNIE: When my brothers and sisters were dying, I wished
them dead all the sooner so as I could have their food.

SEAN: Annie!

ANNIE: I had lots of thoughts like that. Still do. But my
thoughts are wickeder than what I do.

COLONEL: 'Twould be a terrible world if it were the other way
around. I will tell you my secret because you have told
me yours: when I reached the age of twenty – and all this
is over thirty years ago now – I inherited my part of our
father's fortune. I didn't want to spend my life running a
great furniture store in Boston; I wanted to travel, to see
the world. So I was young and rich and very foolish – a
catastrophic combination. I began to gamble – and I was
good, very good – or I thought I was. But within two years

I had gambled away all my money, drunk myself silly on whiskey, and had run into debt. I couldn't pay. I couldn't give up the liquor. I escaped prison by joining the army, where I made a tolerably good soldier. My sisters never forgave me, as I've never forgiven myself. I vowed I would never gamble again, or drink again – and to this day, I have never broken that vow.

ANNIE: But Little Luke found you gambling in the drinking saloon.

COLONEL: Not gambling, or drinking, Annie. Touting for business. I have a casino on board the *Henry Martha*, and I'm always looking to lure gamblers as my passengers. 'Spicable, you might say.

SEAN: Have you never been back to Boston to see Miss Martha and Miss Henry?

COLONEL: I have stood outside the house – the house we were all born in. And I have longed to go inside, but have never dared. I have faced and outfaced English soldiers, Mexicans, Red Indians; but my sister Henry has eyes that reach to my very soul. So I have always walked away, have left Boston without so much as a hello.

ANNIE: Mister Colonel…?

COLONEL: Yes, Annie.

ANNIE: You're not as 'spicable as you like to think.

COLONEL: *(To SEAN.)* Now, young man, you take the wheel.

ANNIE: What about me?

COLONEL: You, Annie: I want you to explore the *Henry Martha* as if she were your own.

* * *

SEAN takes the wheel: the ship's hooter hoots, the paddles rotate into action; ANNIE explores the boat, to the accompaniment of music. Then she comes running to SEAN at the wheel.

ANNIE: Sean, Sean! I seen him! I seen him!

SEAN: Seen who? Father?

ANNIE: No, no. The bounty hunter who stole our torc, I seen him. He's on board, he's gambling in the casino. Come quickly.

COLONEL: Hold fast, young girl. No one comes bursting into my wheelhouse screaming like a wild animal.

ANNIE: But I seen him –

COLONEL: Calm yourself.

ANNIE: The man who took Little Luke and our torc is sitting in your gambling den. Without the torc we will never reach California.

COLONEL: First, it has to be said that this rogue may well have sold your torc already – which may be why he's sitting gambling on my ship. Second, if the torc is in his possession, then it belongs to him –

ANNIE: But third, he stole it.

COLONEL: He would deny it. It would be his word against yours.

ANNIE: And who wouldn't believe me?

COLONEL: Every battle in my experience has to be planned meticulously. The frontal assault would be of no use. We have either to steal it back ourselves, or somehow to winkle it out of him.

ANNIE: So let's steal it.

COLONEL: To steal would be difficult, and even if he does still have it, we don't know where he's hiding it.

He ponders.

There is a way…but you must not interfere nor ask questions of me, no matter what happens. Promise?

SEAN: We promise.

COLONEL: I will begin my campaign tomorrow.

ANNIE: But how do we know your campaign is the right campaign if we don't know what that campaign is?

COLONEL: In my army, Annie, soldiers do not query an officer's orders.

ANNIE: *(Saluting.)* Yes, sir!

COLONEL: Now you dance a jig, soldier – and that's an order!

She does; SEAN fiddles, and this segues into…

*   *   *

The COLONEL sits at a gambling table, opposite the BOUNTY HUNTER.

CARD-DEALER: Gentlemen. This is straight poker. Place your bets.

The COLONEL appears drunk; the BOUNTY HUNTER wins hands down.

SEAN and ANNIE observe unobserved.

ANNIE: *(To SEAN.)* He's gambling. He said he'd never gamble again. And he's drinking whiskey. There is no plan. He's just a drunkard – 'spicable, like Miss Henry said.

SEAN: *(Unsure.)* 'Tis his battle plan, to be sure.

ANNIE: But he's drunk.

SEAN: *(Still unsure.)* I know. But our orders were not to interfere.

The COLONEL loses another hand. The BOUNTY HUNTER rakes in the chips. The COLONEL's pile is low.

BOUNTY HUNTER: You want to give up now, afore you lose everythin'?

COLONEL: I'm only just getting into my stride. Double or quits.

BOUNTY HUNTER: But you have nothing worth gamblin'. I'm not interested in small money.

COLONEL: Then I shall gamble the *Henry Martha*.

General astonishment.

BOUNTY HUNTER: The who?

COLONEL: This paddle-steamer. She's all I have and she's worth a dollar or two.

BOUNTY HUNTER: You're drunk.

COLONEL: That's as maybe, but what do you say? Can you match the bet?

BOUNTY HUNTER: And what might she be worth?

COLONEL: A good few thousand, I'd say.

BOUNTY HUNTER: I got around one thousand here in greenbacks – and I got the rest in gold.

He removes the torc from inside his jacket – to everyone's astonishment.

Are you satisfied, Colonel? Will you play the hand?

COLONEL: I want to touch it first. Feel it.

BOUNTY HUNTER: What?

COLONEL: Your gold thing.

The BOUNTY HUNTER carefully hands it over, suspicious.

No. This is not pure gold. Pure gold would not spring like this.

He bends it.

BOUNTY HUNTER: Careful, man!

COLONEL: It's too dull, too red. It contains an alloy of some kind, copper I should guess. If this is all you have, then I withdraw my offer.

BOUNTY HUNTER: Chicken.

COLONEL: A chicken can lay eggs. She helps to feed people. She is of some use in this world. May I ask if you have ever in all your miserable life done anything as useful? You're a fool, sir, a scavenger and a scoundrel. Do you have something else to match my offer, sir?

BOUNTY HUNTER: That's all I got, Colonel. No more than the clothes I stand up in.

COLONEL: Then I shall take those as well, as an assurance of the bet.

BOUNTY HUNTER: My clothes?

COLONEL: Yup.

BOUNTY HUNTER: You gotta bet. And when I've finished with you here, Colonel, I'll take great pleasure in throwin' you off *my* boat!

COLONEL: So play your hand.

The BOUNTY HUNTER does so with a flourish.

CARD-DEALER: Four Kings and the Ten of Clubs

Gasps.

COLONEL: A good hand. Too good I fear to be an honest hand –

BOUNTY HUNTER: What the…?

COLONEL: But even if it were an honest hand it would not be good enough.

And the COLONEL lays his cards down one by one.

CARD-DEALER: Four Aces and the Queen of Hearts.

More gasps. The BOUNTY HUNTER looks green. The COLONEL is suddenly sober.

COLONEL: You are worse than a dog, sir. You robbed my two young friends here –

SEAN and ANNIE step forward.

BOUNTY HUNTER: You!

COLONEL: You robbed them of everything they had in this world, and that was not much. But now you hand the torc back to them, and you hand them your greenbacks. A bet's a bet.

The BOUNTY HUNTER knows he's been beaten, and hands over the torc and dollar bills.

Aren't you forgetting something?

BOUNTY HUNTER: Colonel?

COLONEL: Your clothes, man, your clothes.

BOUNTY HUNTER: You're kiddin' me!

COLONEL: Jacket, boots, trousers – and what's left of your modesty, I shall throw off *my* ship.

The BOUNTY HUNTER disrobes to roars of laughter.

BOUNTY HUNTER: You cain't do this to me!

But the COLONEL can and so the BOUNTY HUNTER jumps overboard in nothing but his underwear, before he is thrown. The COLONEL throws the BOUNTY HUNTER's clothes overboard after him.

ANNIE: *(To COLONEL.)* You cheated. I saw you under the table. I saw where that Ace of Diamonds came from.

COLONEL: Well that's gratitude for you! Of course I cheated, Annie. I cheated because he cheated. I just did it better, that's all. Did you see where the Ace of *Hearts* came from? You didn't, did you?

ANNIE: But that's dishonest.

COLONEL: What did you want me to do? Lose? You've got your golden torc and the world has righted itself, so what are you grumbling about, young lady?

ANNIE: I'm never grumbling, Mister Colonel. I just wanted you to know that I knew, that's all.

SEAN: Are you sure we're to have all this money, Colonel?

COLONEL: Not all of it, no. We'll need much of it to finance our trip – our wagon, our provisions, our food…

SEAN: 'Our'?

COLONEL: Well you didn't think I'd let you go alone into the wilderness and miss out on the adventure myself, did you? I have always yearned to see the Pacific Ocean before I die. We shall all go West together and find your father.

ANNIE: You don't have to come with us, Mister Colonel. We can manage.

COLONEL: No, I don't *have* to come with you Annie, and I'm sure you would manage. But I *want* to come with you. Now, two thousand miles is a long way to travel – and we cannot go it alone – we're going to have to join a wagon train. We'll need to pick our friends carefully.

SEAN: How will we do that?

COLONEL: We'll hold a meeting.

*   *   *

And a meeting of FARMERS, heading West from a bustling Frontier Town, forms.

My name is Colonel Whitman, Colonel Paul Whitman. You'll be looking for someone to lead your wagons across to California. I have been thinking it over and I'm willing to offer my services.

FARMER: Why you?

COLONEL: You are all farmers. You know your land, you know your stock, you can read the weather from the wind, from the clouds. You know when to plough and when to till.

The FARMERS murmur their assent.

I can do none of those things. But I am – or was – a soldier. My business was to lead men into danger – and to bring them through it. I have also been Captain of a ship. I have to tell you that as a soldier I never lost a battle, and as a ship's Captain I never lost a ship. Those are my qualifications.

FARMER: We need a younger man.

COLONEL: We need young men to drive the wagons and the stock, young men to forage, to hunt and to scout. Every one of you here – man, woman, and child, young and old, has their part to play. Ahead of us lie two thousand miles of some of the worst terrain on earth: scorching plains, flooding rivers, and the deserts. I will get you across it all, if you will let me. As your leader I will have to make harsh decisions on your behalf, decisions you may not approve of, decisions you may not like. But if I lead you, I make the rules. I know no other way to command. I don't expect you to like me. But I do expect to reach California, with all of you – alive.

FARMER/MATT COLBY: That's straight talkin', Colonel. I'm Matt Colby, farmer from Illinois, and I surely like what I hear. You get my vote. We got all the wagons we need. We got all our cattle. We got our families. And I wanna be first on the trail, first to the grazing, first to every water hole. I don't want the prairies eaten and hunted out in front of us. I don't wanna eat dust for two thousand miles. I say we puts our trust in this Colonel and makes him our Captain.

The FARMERS voice their assent.

COLONEL: I thank you Matt Colby, friends; I thank you for your confidence. We should leave at dawn. And we should post a sentry at every fourth wagon as we await sunrise. Tomorrow when we leave, I want two tight lines of wagons. No stragglers. If you have got a problem with a wheel and a shaft, you let the out-riders know and they'll tell me. We'll be leaving no one behind. And we shall want two men to ride upfront with the guide – we do have a guide, I hope?

FRENCH CHARLIE steps forward.

FRENCH CHARLIE: Charlie Charbonnier: French Charlie they call me.

COLONEL: Well, French Charlie, here's the rules: no one leaves the camp alone at night; no one goes unarmed outside the perimeter of the corral; and no alcohol – water is our fuel. Fill the barrels to the brim, Mr Colby.

FRENCH CHARLIE: No whiskey?

COLONEL: No whiskey. Guns and whiskey do not mix. Whiskey saps a man and we shall need all our strength to reach California. Now, goodnight to you all: to your beds and sleep well. We've an early start tomorrow.

The FARMERS leave.

SEAN: Well, that was quite something, Colonel.

ANNIE: I didn't know your name was Paul.

COLONEL: You never asked. Now you take a blanket and sleep, both of you.

SEAN: But I'm too excited to sleep.

COLONEL: Lie down and look up at the stars.

They do so. Quiet, apart from the cicadas.

(In a lullaby voice.) Always a source of wonder to me, children, that up there somewhere in the stars could be an old Colonel looking right up at us and saying to his children: 'Always a source of wonder to me, children, that up there somewhere in the stars could be an old Colonel looking right up at us and saying to his children: "Always a source of wonder to me, children, that up there somewhere …".'

And they have fallen asleep.

*   *   *

Dawn. The braying of horses. The lowing of cattle. The preparations of the wagon train. FRENCH CHARLIE approaches.

FRENCH CHARLIE: Morning, Colonel.

COLONEL: French Charlie. You will ride out a mile ahead of the column and send back a scout to report any problems to me – Indians, river crossings. I reckon we should be travelling fifteen, twenty miles a day, all being well.

FRENCH CHARLIE: You'll be lucky.

COLONEL: I hope so, Mr Charbonnier. Now, Mr Colby, we have a heck of a way to go, so let them wagons roll!

Yee-hah! And they're off. SEAN plays a jig to set them on their way.

* * *

The journey passes – hot, dusty – and passes some more. Music. Weeks, months go by and are endured.

MATT COLBY serves up the water from the barrel – equal ladles to each.

FRENCH CHARLIE: I'll have some more water, if you please.

MATT COLBY looks at the COLONEL.

COLONEL: Mr Charbonnier?

FRENCH CHARLIE: I work harder than the others. 'Sonly right.

COLONEL: If you take more than your fair share, then that means there's less for the next person – and none for the next. No one will have more than his ration. We survive only if we share.

FRENCH CHARLIE draws a gun on the COLONEL.

FRENCH CHARLIE: I suggest you change your mind, Colonel.

The COLONEL draws his gun on FRENCH CHARLIE.

COLONEL: If you force me to shoot you, I will.

A THIRD MAN draws his gun on the COLONEL.

THIRD MAN/BOUNTY HUNTER: I bin' meanin' to catch up with you, Colonel.

The BOUNTY HUNTER spies the CHILDREN.

BOUNTY HUNTER: Well, lookee who's here. Now I got a nice surprise for you. French Charlie here wanted to kill you all, but I said no, that ain't right. We'll just leave 'em out here in the middle of nowhere without a drop of water. An' French Charlie agreed. Now ain't that just fine? Course, 'fore we leave, I'd be obliged if you'd open that fiddle case of your'n young man, and hand me that gold necklet.

SEAN: I won't!

COLONEL: Do as he says, Sean.

SEAN reluctantly does as he says.

BOUNTY HUNTER: You'll have to kill me to get this off me again. An' you ain't about to do that, is you? 'Fraid we ain't got no water to spare – a man dries out slowly in the sun…

FRENCH CHARLIE: *(Addressing MATT COLBY.)* Now yous all be comin' with us. I'm the only one knows the way through this wilderness. And you can drink as much whiskey as you like to help you through.

ANNIE: *(Railing at BOUNTY HUNTER.)* You take our torc with you, Mister, an' you'll die. 'Tis the O'Brien torc.

BOUNTY HUNTER: We all gotta die, girl.

MATT COLBY: I'm staying with the Colonel and the children.

FRENCH CHARLIE: We ain't leaving you no water. You gotta know that.

MATT COLBY: I reckons I got more chance with the Colonel than yous got without him.

COLONEL: No, Matt. You go with them. He's the only one knows the way out of this hell. He's your best hope.

MATT COLBY: But Colonel –

COLONEL: That's an order, soldier.

MATT COLBY: Colonel. Take my drinking bottle.

COLONEL: I will. Thank you. Now you get along back to your family – there'll be someone along the trail to relieve us afore too long. On your way now.

MATT COLBY leaves with the BOUNTY HUNTER and FRENCH CHARLIE.

We'll not be downhearted, will we? Remember California – less than a week or so over those mountains. I'm very sorry you lost the torc after all you've been through – but you've lost it before and got it back. We may have lost the battle, but the war is still to be won.

ANNIE: Will we be travelling on?

COLONEL: Yes we will. While there's a full moon, we'll travel in the cool of the night – save our water. Rest up by day; march at night. Will you play something, set us off to rest til' nightfall, Sean?

He plays something melancholic. ANNIE rests. When SEAN has finished playing, he sleeps too. The COLONEL takes a long look at them, checks that they have the water bottle and then walks off into the desert, alone.

* * *

The moon rises. ANNIE awakes.

ANNIE: Mister Colonel! Where are you Mister Colonel?

SEAN awakes.

SEAN: What is it Annie?

ANNIE: The Colonel. He's gone.

SEAN: Where has he gone?

ANNIE: He's left us the water. I think he's gone in order to save us. He's left us so that we can march on with the water, helping us that little bit further.

SEAN: But we can't go on. I can't go on. I have no strength in me any more, Annie.

ANNIE: *(Shaking him by the shoulders.)* We'll not be giving up, Sean. Not after what the Colonel has done for us. We have to try, Sean. For the Colonel's sake. We have to try.

SEAN: Oh, Annie. I think you're right. Perhaps we should follow the Colonel?

ANNIE: There is no trail to follow.

SEAN: Shouldn't we try to find him?

ANNIE: Like he said, we've a heck of a way to go.

There's a growl.

SEAN: What was that?

The growl is even louder, closer.

ANNIE: I'm not sure. But I'm not staying to find out.

And they exit, pursued by a BEAR.

* * *

Dawn. SEAMUS FINN looks down across the desert from the trees, through a telescope.

SEAMUS FINN: *(To himself.)* A graveyard of a place. Sure, there's not a bear fool enough to set a foot out there. *(Raises his voice to the non-existent bear.)* You cost me a week of me life, you divil! I been trackin' you for a week now. Don't think you've seen the last of me, mister bear. You may have got away this time, but there's always the next time.

He puts his telescope to his eye for one last look – and spots something unexpected.

(Crossing himself.) Jasus, Mary Mother of God. Will you look what is out there? Will you just look. What the divil's a young boy like that doing out there all on his own? Don't I have enough troubles without addin' to them? No gold, no bears in my traps, and now this? 'Tis not fair on a man, not fair at all.

SEAMUS makes his way towards SEAN and ANNIE.

An' where the divil did you come from, young man? An' who is that you have with you?

SEAN: 'Tis my sister, Annie, and she's near dying, mister, for want of water. Would you have some water, mister?

SEAMUS FINN: To be sure I have, young man.

He hands SEAN his canteen and SEAN pours the water onto ANNIE's parched lips. As the water trickles down her throat, she coughs herself back to life.

SEAN: Thank you, mister.

SEAMUS FINN: Sure, 'tis nothing. An' I should say you are about as lost as a young man could be. By the talk of you, you would be an Irishman, would you not? No, but 'tis not possible. 'Tis years since I heard those dulcet tones from a man. 'Bout here they grunt and spit more'n they talk. There's no one speaks English as sweet as an Irishman. An' that's an Irish smile you're wearin'. You're never Irish, young man, are you?

SEAN: *(Smiling.)* County Cork!

SEAMUS FINN: *(Laughing.)* Kerry! I'm Seamus Finn from Kerry. Jasus, Mary Mother of God, it can't be true. Out here in the middle of nothin' and I run into a lad from County Cork! An' would she be from County Cork too?

ANNIE: 'Course I am. I'm his sister, am I not?

SEAMUS FINN: Sure you are, darlin' – an' welcome back to the land of the livin'.

SEAN takes a big glug of water.

Now, when your brother's finished my water, then I'll see yous both be gettin' out of this terrible place. You'll be on your own, I suppose?

They say nothing.

I suppose so then. *(To ANNIE.)* Can you walk, or shall I be carryin' you?

He doesn't wait for an answer and picks ANNIE up and carries her.

And to think I nearly didn't see you. If it hadn't been for the bear that I've not seen or heard…maybe it was meant. I've been talkin' to nothin' but the birds and beasts and a few Indians –

SEAN: Indians?

SEAMUS FINN: Sure – no one but these creatures for ten years or more. Been trappin' up here all that time. Bears. Met a Russian or two, a few Frenchmen. And I've known the odd American: you see them all down at the Fort where I take my bear skins for trading. But in all this time I've never met another proper Irishman. Jasus, Mary Mother of God, I think I could die of happiness.

ANNIE: Don't die, mister.

SEAMUS FINN: Oh, I won't die 'til I'm entirely happy.

SEAN: What would make you happy?

SEAMUS FINN: Gold.

SEAN: Gold?

SEAMUS FINN: Gold. The fur trade's all but finished, you know.

ANNIE: No, I don't know.

SEAMUS FINN: The creatures are scarcer now and more wily. So it's gold I've been after these past two summers. An' all I find is fool's gold, by the bucketful. An' now you. But I wasn't lookin' for you, now, was I?

He puts ANNIE down.

I suppose it would be too much to hope that one of you plays that fiddle?

ANNIE: Sean plays it.

SEAN gets the fiddle out of its case.

SEAMUS FINN: What a fine instrument, a fine sight indeed. An' would you want to play it for me, young man? 'Twould stop old Seamus Finn from prattling on, now, would it not?

SEAN raises the violin to his chin – then lowers it.

SEAN: Mr Finn. My heart would not be in it. Fiddler Donnelly – him that taught me how to play it – he said you should never play the fiddle if your heart's not in it. I'm thinking I won't ever have the heart for it again.

ANNIE: We've lost our mother, Mr Finn. And the golden torc, the ancient saviour of the O'Briens. We've lost our friends in shipwrecks, waved goodbye to people we'll never see again – and now we've lost the Colonel too, out there in the desert. We be looking for our father, out West in California. But now I fear we've lost him too.

SEAMUS FINN: But we are out West, on the edge of California.

SEAN: We are?

SEAMUS FINN: For sure we are. And you'll not need that torc of yours if she be lost.

ANNIE: Why not, Mr Finn?

SEAMUS FINN: Can you not see: 'tis nothing short of a miracle that you have survived to tell this tale. The torc has worked this miracle for you. But now, you won't be needin' it no more.

SEAN: I don't know…

SEAMUS FINN: Well I do. There's nothin' at all to be sad about. Sure, that Fiddler of yours wouldn't want you to stop fiddlin', now, would he? It's the fiddle too that has kept you alive in this beautiful world. Your friends gave their lives so you could live, and will you repay them now by grievin'? No. After a fine life, back home in Ireland, do we not hold a wake? Do we not dance and sing? We do not mope! We do not weep! Never! So now, right now, we'll hold a wake and we'll dance and we'll sing. Take the fiddle, Sean O'Brien, for that's your name – and make music! And all the Angels will sing.

SEAN plays his fiddle – tentatively, melancholy at first, then faster, stronger, happier – and ANNIE and SEAMUS FINN dance together. All the ANGELS sing.

ANNIE: Mr Finn. Would you take us to find our father?

SEAMUS FINN: No bother, darlin', no bother at all. But first you can help me with my pannin' –

SEAN: 'Pannin''?

SEAMUS FINN: Panning for gold.

ANNIE: I thought you said we didn't need gold no more?

SEAMUS FINN: You do not. But I surely do.

SEAN: How do you pan for gold?

SEAMUS FINN: Sure there's nothin' to it. *(He demonstrates.)* You just shovel the pay dirt from the river bank into the frying pan, take out the few sticks, add a touch of water and swirl it round so that the soil is taken off by the water. The gold, when you find it, will lie heavy and stay in the bottom of the pan. You'll notice it for sure for 'tis yellow as the sun and will glow at you. Sure, 'tis simplicity itself. Nothin' to it.

ANNIE: Then why haven't you found any, Seamus Finn, seeing as it's that simple?

Pause.

SEAMUS FINN: You have a cruel tongue for such a pretty girl. Do you not cut to the quick? There's hundreds of folk diggin' away down-river, but they don't know what I know. No one does. 'Tis me secret… *(His lips are sealed – but he's bursting to tell his secret.)* But I'll share it with you because

I've been longin' to share it with someone I can trust, an' there's not many of them about. Two years ago, an old Indian chief came by while I was camping by the river an' he told me I would find gold, so much gold that I'd be the richest man in the world. He told me there was so much of it that the water ran yellow from the mountain! A man believes what he wants to believe. So I built me cabin and for two hot summers long I've dug an' I've panned. 'Tis here, I know 'tis here. I feel it in me nose. But I've not been able to find it. Not yet. Now, with two extra pairs of fresh young eyes on the job we could snap up a fortune, a mighty fortune. And I could be off back home to Ireland where I belong – but I'll not go back a poor man: I'll return with enough money to buy half of Kerry, or I'll not go back at all.

He shoves a frying pan into each of their hands, and they get panning. SEAMUS FINN moves upstream.

(Muttering when there's nothing in his pan again.) Damn, damn, damn and damnation!

ANNIE: Listen.

SEAN: 'Tis only Seamus cursing again, Annie.

The rumble of horses' hooves.

ANNIE: Not Seamus. Listen.

The horses' hooves thunder – there's the whooping of RED INDIANS, and SEAN and ANNIE run like gazelles to SEAMUS FINN.

ANNIE + SEAN: Seamus! Seamus! Seamus Finn!

SEAMUS FINN: An' what are you two hollerin' about, you little divils?

SEAN + ANNIE: Indians! Indians! Indians!

SEAMUS FINN: Will you stop your nonsense! Stop your hollerin'! You'll frighten them away.

SEAN: *We'll* frighten *them*?

SEAMUS FINN: They'll not be hurtin' you. They're just Indians, friends of mine, you might say. The old chief I was tellin' you about – every time he sets eyes on me, he laughs until he cries, the old divil.

And sure enough, the INDIANS led by their RED INDIAN CHIEF are there bent double, consumed by laughter.

(To ANNIE + SEAN.) Will you just stay where you are, an' there'll be no trouble. They need to know whether you're a friend or an enemy. There's nothing much in between. They've been here for ever and now we've all turned up and are taking their land. If they get in the ways, too many of them get killed, and so they fight back, who can blame 'em?

ANNIE: Well, we're friends, not enemies.

SEAMUS FINN: Of course you are, but they don't know that yet.

SEAMUS FINN approaches the RED INDIAN CHIEF. They greet each other with a ritual – then the RED INDIAN CHIEF laughs. He speaks perfect English, much to SEAN and ANNIE's surprise.

RED INDIAN CHIEF: Good evening, Mr Finn. And how is your hunt for gold coming along?

SEAMUS FINN: Very well, thank you. And how is yourself?

RED INDIAN CHIEF: I could not be better. In fact I have a proposition for you.

SEAMUS FINN: You do, do you?

RED INDIAN CHIEF: Yes indeedy-do-dah. One of the tribe witnessed an attack two days ago by an elegant-looking migrant on two seedy-looking men from a beleaguered, forlorn, and chaotic mess of a wagon-train.

SEAN: The Colonel and the bounty hunter and French Charlie!

RED INDIAN CHIEF: They were arguing about something or whatnot and all ended up killing each other. One of the seedy men was wearing a twist of gold beneath his jerkin.

ANNIE: Oh, Sean. The Colonel died trying to get back our torc from the bounty hunter.

RED INDIAN CHIEF: I have no use for gold, as you know. But you have been searching for gold for a 'divil' of a long time, so I was wondering if you would like to buy this gold from me.

SEAMUS FINN: Buy?

RED INDIAN CHIEF: Exchange it for some of your bear-skins.

SEAMUS FINN: Let me see this gold of yours.

The RED INDIAN CHIEF brandishes the golden torc.

ANNIE: Sean!

SEAN: *(To ANNIE.)* Sh!

SEAMUS FINN: *(Rubbing his chin.)* No, that's not the kind of gold I'm after.

ANNIE: Seamus Finn!

SEAN gives ANNIE a prod with his elbow.

SEAMUS FINN: No. Gold's worth little if it's been fashioned for the white man's vanity. It's raw gold I'm after, pure gold.

RED INDIAN CHIEF: Well, if you change your mind…

ANNIE can contain herself no longer.

ANNIE: Buy it, Mr Finn, no matter what the cost. 'Tis our torc, you can't let it go. Men have died trying to save it for us. We'll pay you back.

The RED INDIAN CHIEF smiles. SEAMUS FINN's shoulders slump.

SEAMUS FINN: Oh, Annie. Do you imagine I didn't know it was your torc and that you'd want it back? I was just about to persuade the old divil that it might be worth a few pelts, nothing more. The last thing I wanted was for him to know we'd pay him the earth for it. Annie, you're the sweetest thing, but when it comes to matters of business you've got the brain of a donkey.

RED INDIAN CHIEF: So I suggest that you give me your entire collection of pelts, Mr Finn. You will not find a golden torc like this every day of the week, believe me. And you would not want to disappoint the young lady, now, would you?

SEAMUS FINN reluctantly hands over his pile of skins – and the RED INDIAN CHIEF hands over the golden torc to ANNIE.

ANNIE: Thank you, Seamus; thank you sir.

The RED INDIAN CHIEF pulls a fierce face.

RED INDIAN CHIEF: Boo!

And he laughs and leaves with the other INDIANS.

SEAMUS FINN: *(To ANNIE.)* You'll be the ruin of me.

ANNIE: I'm sorry.

SEAMUS FINN: Never be sorry for what's past. Let's just call it a little *disaster*. Be happy, and think to the future.

ANNIE: Can we go and find Father now?

SEAMUS FINN: Well, there's little else for us to stay for. So why not?

SEAN: What shall we do with our pans?

SEAMUS FINN: We'll wash them out one last time, and then we'll pack them away for good.

They wash the pans out – and SEAN stares at what he finds in the bottom of his.

SEAN: Annie. Could I be looking at the torc please? Would you let me have it a moment?

ANNIE hands it over.

ANNIE: I don't want it anyway. It's killed many a good man and ruined others. It has a curse on it, Sean, I know it has.

SEAMUS FINN: It's not me day, is it? I'm getting old, that's what be happenin'. I only look in the mirror once a year – a man keeps younger that way; or maybe he just thinks he does. No gold, no pelts, and now no fun with you twos.

SEAN: Oh, I don't know Seamus. Will you take a look at what I've found.

And he reveals a golden nugget the size of his fist, shaped like a jagged boot. SEAMUS FINN stares in wonder. He can hardly bring himself to touch it. Then he picks it up and cradles it like an egg.

SEAMUS FINN: Holy Mary, Mother of God.

He falls to his knees.

(To SEAN + ANNIE.) Oh you darlins, you little darlins! I've seen enough fool's gold to know that this is the real thing!

SEAN: And there's plenty more where that came from – a whole streak of gold along the river bed.

SEAMUS FINN: Forget Kerry! There'll be enough to buy all of Ireland! But I'm not a greedy man. Half of Ireland will do!

They pack up their gold and violin case and so on, and make their way to Grass Valley.

* * *

So we'll head for Grass Valley. It's where all the most hopeful emigrants go in California.

ANNIE: Why?

SEAMUS FINN: Because there was not supposed to be grass in the desert – and yet in California, anything is possible.

Grass Valley. People.

Beggin' your pardon, sir, but we're lookin' for one Patrick O'Brien, lately arrived from Ireland.

MAN: I don't know no O'Brien. But the Irish are further down Grass Valley, towards the sea.

SEAMUS FINN: Much obliged.

They walk on some more.

Beggin' your pardon, sir, but we're lookin' for a Patrick O'Brien, who lives in these here parts.

ANOTHER MAN: O'Brien… O'Brien… Nope. Plenty of Paddys, but can't recall an O'Brien. Ask at the stores, they might've heard of him.

So they go on to the stores.

SEAMUS FINN: Beggin' your pardon, Ma'am, but we're lookin' for one Patrick O'Brien, lately come from County Cork in Ireland. D'you know the man I'm speaking of by any chance?

WOMAN: Sure I do, sir.

SEAMUS FINN: You do?

ANNIE and SEAN are overjoyed.

WOMAN: His place is a short while down along Grass Valley. It's the only house you'll find. Built himself a fine place he has, tallest chimney I ever did see. But I ain't seen him for a couple of months now, not since he came back. Are you kin of his maybe?

ANNIE: We are!

SEAN: Son and daughter.

ANNIE: He's the son and I'm the daughter.

WOMAN: I can tell that right enough! Keep along the river this side of the bank, and you can't miss it.

SEAMUS FINN: Ma'am. I'll be needin' a horse an' saddle. I see you've some fine animals in the paddock. I'll pay you well – in gold, proper gold.

WOMAN: You mean real, live gold?

SEAMUS FINN: Yes Ma'am. I'll be needin' a mount to take me so far as San Francisco.

ANNIE: Will you be leaving us, Seamus?

SEAMUS FINN: I'll not be delayin' you much longer, we've come to the parting of our ways. Your way lies ahead and my way to the south, to San Francisco.

ANNIE: Please stay with us, at least till we find Father again.

SEAMUS FINN: I've made up me mind. You'll not be needin' me any more now, will you? So I'll be goin' on my way – but I'd like you to have somethin' before I go.

He hands them the gold.

SEAN: But that's all your gold, Seamus!

SEAMUS FINN: Not quite all, but almost, for sure. Why would I need it when I get back to Ireland?

SEAN: To buy half of Kerry, like you said.

SEAMUS FINN: I'm not so certain Kerry is for sale, and I'm gettin' on. Old men grow no younger. You're both still very young. You could do with the gold more than me.

ANNIE: But we have our golden torc.

SEAMUS FINN: You surely have. And you must treasure it.

SEAN: 'Tis your gold, Seamus. Didn't you come to America to make your fortune? And didn't we come to find our father? And haven't we all found our pot of gold?

SEAMUS FINN: Sure, 'tis nothing. Give it to your father. As more people come, the cost of land and beasts will soon be a match for that gold.

ANNIE: Thank you, Seamus.

SEAMUS FINN: Consider it a parting gift to the prettiest girl in the world.

He wipes away a tear.

Now I'll be on my way before you unman me.

SEAN: Goodbye, Seamus Finn.

ANNIE: Goodbye.

SEAMUS FINN: *(Leaving.)* Never look back, children, never look back.

And he's gone. Silence. The sound of the sea.

ANNIE: Let's go home, Sean.

SEAN: Yes, let's go home.

And they run towards a house with a tall chimney –

ANNIE: Look: a tall chimney. It must be Father's!

SEAN: Do you think Father'll recognise us?

ANNIE: *(Running.)* He'll tell me I've grown, and he'll pick me up and throw me into the air, catch me under the arms and swing me high again –

– but they are suddenly stopped in their tracks. A newly dug grave: a crude wooden cross, crooked in the ground.

Oh, Sean!

And they fall to their knees, wailing and keening.

He's dead, he's dead, he's dead.

A MAN approaches, silhouetted against the setting sun.

MAN: And what might you ragamuffins be wanting? 'Tis almost sundown. Is it a bed you're after?

SEAN and ANNIE are dumbfounded.

Have you not got tongues in those heads of yours?

SEAN: Do you not recognise us?

Pause.

ANNIE: Do you not know who we are, Father?

And now the MAN is dumbfounded.

SEAN: Father?

Pause.

MAN/FATHER: Annie? Sean?

SEAN: And is it really you?

They hug.

You gave us a terrible fright. The grave.

FATHER: Oh, for sure 'tis sad. 'Tis our old dog, Caitlin. She followed me back East and across the seas to Ireland to fetch you, and when you weren't there she followed me all the way back West to California again. Worn out with living – died only last week.

ANNIE: We thought it was you, Father.

And the three of them hug some more.

WOMAN'S VOICE: *(Off.)* Patrick O'Brien! Are you comin' with that wood for the oven or aren't you? Do I fetch it myself?

FATHER: I'm comin' – and bringin' you something better than wood.

The WOMAN – MOTHER steps into the setting sunlight, silhouetted.

MOTHER: Annie? Sean?

They are dumbfounded again.

Is it you?

SEAN + ANNIE: Mother?!

MOTHER: Am I dreamin'?

SEAN: Not unless we are – and we're not dreamin', are we Annie?

ANNIE: I don't know, Sean. If it is dreamin', then don't wake me up.

And they all hug.

MOTHER: It is a miracle! I thought you were dead.

SEAN: And we thought you'd died too.

MOTHER: A fine bunch of maudlin O'Briens we are.

FATHER: I missed you by moments. I docked as your ship set sail for 'Merica. Your Mother was dying but waiting for me, and she told me about the English soldier and how he saved you, and when she got better, we followed you as

soon as we could – but we got back here and never spied
you on the way. We'd given you both up for dead.

ANNIE: Dead? When we had the torc to protect us?

FATHER: You still have the torc?

ANNIE: It's worked terrible hard to get us here.

She reveals the golden torc in all its glory.

MOTHER: And you too, my children, you must have worked
terrible hard too.

SEAN: Oh, we had others to help us.

ANNIE: Yes: Fiddler Donnelly and Mr Blundell –

SEAN: – and Miss Henry and Miss Martha, and Little Luke –

ANNIE: – and the Colonel and –

SEAN: – Seamus Finn…

FATHER: And who might they all be?

MOTHER: And where did you come by that old fiddle case,
Sean?

FATHER: And when did you two grow up so?

MOTHER: And have you been washing your neck, Sean
O'Brien?

SEAN: Mother!

MOTHER: Tell us all.

Pause.

SEAN: Well, 'tis a long story, Mother. A long, long story.

*And he takes out the fiddle and plays the heartiest reel and ANNIE
dances, and MOTHER and FATHER too, and they all live happily
ever after…*

The End.

OTHER ADAPTATIONS BY SIMON READE

Pride and Prejudice
Jane Austen
£8.99 / 9781840029512

The Scarecrow and His Servant
Phillip Pullman
£8.99 / 9781840028997

Not the End of the World
Geraldine McCaughrean
£8.99 / 9781840027365

Private Peaceful & Other Plays
(Private Peaceful / Aladdin and the Enchanted Lamp /
The Owl Who Was Afraid of the Dark)
Michael Morpurgo, Phillip Pullman, Jill Tomlinson
£9.99 / 9781840026603

OTHER TITLES BY SIMON READE

Dear Mr Shakespeare:
Letters to a Jobbing Playwright
£9.99 / 9781840028294

WWW.OBERONBOOKS.COM

Follow us on www.twitter.com/@oberonbooks
& www.facebook.com/oberonbook